The House and Foreign Policy

CHARLES W. WHALEN, JR.

The House and Foreign Policy

The Irony of Congressional Reform

The University of North Carolina Press   Chapel Hill

This publication was prepared under a
grant from the Woodrow Wilson International Center
for Scholars, Washington, D.C.
The statements and views expressed
herein are those of the author and are
not necessarily those of the Wilson Center.

Library of Congress Cataloging in Publication Data

Whalen, Charles W., Jr.
The House and foreign policy.

Includes bibliographical references and index.
1. United States. Congress. House. 2. Legislation—United States. 3. United States—Foreign
relations. I. Title.
JK1081.W47   328.73′072   81-16342
ISBN 0-8078-1515-2   AACR2
ISBN 0-8078-4088-2 (pbk.)

Contents

Tables

Acknowledgments

Legislative and constituent demands upon a congressman leave him little time for reflection. During my first eleven years in the House of Representatives I was not immune to this dilemma. In my last year (1978), however, freed from the pressures of running for re-election, I accepted an invitation from the Capitol Historical Society to teach graduate courses in congressional processes and Congress and foreign policy. This forced me to study Congress as an institution in a much more intensive and objective way than I had previously been able to do. This detailed review convinced me that the House's foreign-policy actions, which I found very disturbing, were directly linked to the changes in that chamber's rules effected during the previous seven years. Upon leaving Congress in 1979, I received a fellowship from the Woodrow Wilson International Center for Scholars which enabled me to put those conclusions into writ. g

I am especially grateful to Dr. James H. Billington, director, and Dr. Michael J. Lacey, secretary of the program on American society and politics, for the encouragement that they extended me during my ten months at the Wilson Center. My research assistants, Anthony Garofola and Kimberley Groome, rendered invaluable service in securing necessary background and supporting data, as did James Blakely and his associates at my "other office," the Madison Congressional Reading Room of the Library of Congress. To Genevieve Weiler and Patricia Sheridan, who translated my sometimes illegible script into a readable manuscript, goes my sincere appreciation.

I also am indebted to the following individuals who so kindly took the time to review all, or portions, of my original draft and whose comments and constructive suggestion have been so helpful: George Berdes, Dr. I. M. Destler, Clifford Hackett, Representative Gillis W. Long (D.-La.), Timothy Lovain, former assistant secretary of state C. William Maynes, Dr. Norman Ornstein, Thomas Popovich, Thomas Snitch, William Steponkus, and former ambassador H. G. Torbert, Jr.

Finally, my thanks go to Lewis Bateman, executive editor of the University of North Carolina Press, for his willingness to encourage his board of directors to publish this book and to my editor, David Perry, who has done so much to improve the style and readability of my manuscript.

The House and Foreign Policy

CHAPTER 1

A Reassertive House

Promptly at nine o'clock on the evening of January 12, 1977, Doorkeeper James T. Molloy swung open the center doors of the House of Representatives and intoned the familiar introduction, which inevitably evokes a stir of excitement among those who gather to hear a State of the Union Message, "Mr. Speaker: The President of the United States."

Defeated the previous November in his quest to retain his presidency, Gerald R. Ford was making his last official appearance in a chamber where he had served for almost a quarter of a century. American voters, who biennially returned a Democratic majority to the House of Representatives, had denied Ford his dream of becoming speaker. Instead, a series of historical quirks had thrust him into the nation's highest political office.

As I watched Jerry Ford, escorted by a committee of senators and representatives, approach the dais, I thought back to the afternoon of October 10, 1973. On that day I was standing just off the House floor in the speaker's lobby when a reporter approached me and inquired, "Have you read the ticker tape? Agnew has just resigned." After making a quick check of the Associated Press wire to verify this, I rushed to the House floor to tell Ford. Reaching the minority leader's desk just ahead of me was Congressman Elford A. Cederberg (R.-Mich.), who exclaimed, "Jerry, Spiro Agnew just resigned." Ford, obviously startled by the news, replied, "I don't believe it." I assured him Cederberg's report was accurate. Thus began Gerald Ford's strange odyssey to 1600 Pennsylvania Avenue.

Executive Concerns

Like many of his predecessors, President Ford used his "farewell" speech to advise the Congress as to the course it should follow in the future, and he particularly expressed the hope that "this new Congress [would] reexamine its constitutional role in international affairs." Concerned about the growing differences over foreign policy between the executive and legislative branches, Ford observed:

> The exclusive right to declare war, the duty to advise and consent on the part of the Senate, and the power of the purse on the part of the House are ample authority for the legislative branch and should be jealously guarded. But because we may have been too careless of these powers in the past does not justify Congressional intrusion into, or obstruction of, the proper exercise of Presidential responsibilities now or in the future. There can be only one Commander-in-Chief. In these times crises cannot be managed and wars cannot be waged by committee. Nor can peace be pursued solely by parliamentary debate. To the ears of the world, the President speaks for the Nation. While he is, of course, ultimately accountable to the Congress, the courts, and the people, he and his emissaries must not be handicapped in advance in their relations with foreign governments as has sometimes happened in the past.[1]

Ford's remarks echoed the oft-expressed views of his secretary of state, Henry M. Kissinger, who had been exposed to the sting of congressional "intrusion" as early as 1969 when he was appointed President Nixon's assistant for national security affairs. In a year-end (1974) interview appearing in *Business Week*, Kissinger called for a détente between the two branches of government.

> We have to come to an understanding with the Congress about the proper relationship between the executive and legislative functions. What Congress should legislate and what should be left to executive discretion. The attempt to prescribe every detail of policy by congressional action can, over a period of time, so stultify flexibility that you have no nego-

tiating room left at all. We recognize that Congress must exercise ultimate policy. . . . I would hope that the Congress would keep in mind that we need some flexibility.[2]

A Resurgent Congress

As he read that section of his address proposing congressional abjuration of its foreign-policy "obstructionism," President Ford triggered another memory—this time of our telephone conversation of August 20, 1974. Earlier that year, Representative Lee H. Hamilton (D.-Ind.) and I had organized a bipartisan "ad hoc" group of twenty-one members of the House Foreign Affairs Committee to review the Fiscal Year 1975 Foreign Aid Authorization Bill.*

During our periodic luncheon discussions in my office we drafted twenty-eight amendments to that measure, twenty-five of which the committee adopted during its "mark-up sessions."† Among those

---

*Implementation of a congressional program usually involves two steps. First, the plan must be "authorized" by the committee of appropriate jurisdiction. Foreign aid, for instance, comes within the purview of the House Foreign Affairs Committee. The authorization bill spells out the purposes of the program and how it will be conducted, and sets a spending ceiling for each of its principal parts (foreign aid is broken down into such categories as military credit sales, development assistance, and the Peace Corps).

Next, an appropriations bill must be enacted before funds can be drawn by the Treasury Department to finance the projects embodied in the authorization measure. The appropriations bill is initially considered in the relevant subcommittee of the Appropriations Committee (in the case of foreign aid it is the Subcommittee on Foreign Operations), and the subcommittee's recommendations are then acted upon by the full committee. Often the monies actually appropriated for an authorized program are less than the sum permitted in the authorization bill. In some instances a project has never "gotten off the ground" because of the Appropriations Committee's refusal to fund it.

†The term *mark-up* refers to the process by which a committee drafts a bill. The working document is either an informal proposal (usually prepared by the executive branch or the committee chairman) or a measure that has already been formally introduced in the House (and thus bears a number) by the chairman or other members. It is considered paragraph by paragraph. As each section is read, amendments are entertained, discussed, and disposed of by voice vote, a show of hands, or a roll call. After all sections have been considered, the bill, as amended, is put to a final vote by the chairman. If approved, a "clean" bill usually is dropped in the "hopper"

amendments accepted by the committee was one of mine which reduced postwar reconstruction assistance for Indochina by $366.4 million. President Ford, who at that time had occupied the White House for only eleven days, called me to urge that I withdraw it. I declined to do so for reasons that I outlined four days later in a column in the *Washington Post*: "The committee properly avoided a new and indefinite commitment (i.e., economic development) which, under present and foreseeable future circumstances, cannot be met."[3]

The Hamilton-Whalen coalition was but one instance of the growing assertiveness of the House of Representatives in the process of decision making in foreign policy during the 1970s. Few presidential avenues escaped congressional roadblocks. For example, legislation enacted between 1970 and 1979 prohibited the use of military and covert forces in certain situations; reserved to Congress the right to veto certain arms sales abroad; instructed United States delegates to certain international institutions how to vote on various matters coming before their bodies; enjoined economic assistance that supported the processing and marketing of metals and agricultural commodities that compete with American products; banned aid to a select list of Third World Communist states; reduced or denied grants and loans to countries adjudged to have violated internationally recognized human-rights standards; and precluded extension of the "most-favored-nation" (MFN) clause to several trading partners.

Another phenomenon of the last decade was the growing tendency on the part of members of Congress to become involved in international negotiations. In some instances this was mandated by statute; in others it was the result of executive-branch invitation. But there also were a number of personal diplomatic initiatives. On June 27, 1979, for example, when the United States ambassador to Nicaragua arrived in the office of that country's president, General Anastasio Debayle Somoza, to urge him to resign, he was shocked to see Representative John M. Murphy (D.-N.Y.), chairman of the House Merchant Marine and Fisheries Committee, at the general's

---

on the House floor by the chairman. It contains the names of any other committee members who wish to be listed as cosponsors. The staff then prepares a committee report which accompanies the measure as it progresses through the Rules Committee and floor debate.

side. In October and November 1979, Congressman George Hansen (R.-Ida.) visited Teheran in the hope of securing the release of the American hostages held captive there by Iranian militants.

Indeed, during the 1970s our country witnessed what authors Thomas M. Franck and Edward Weisband termed a foreign-policy "revolution," one which "radically redistributed the power of government."[4] Agreeing with this assessment was William D. Rogers, former assistant secretary and undersecretary of state (1974–76). In a September 9, 1979, *New York Times* article, Rogers wrote that "foreign policy has become almost synonymous with law-making. The result is to place a straitjacket of legislation around the manifold complexity of our relations with other nations."[5]

That revolution in the making of foreign policy is the main concern of this book. Along the way we shall consider what precipitated the congressional rebellion, who the leaders of the uprising were and what weapons they employed, what previously unavailable legislative powers were used, and, most important, how foreign policy was affected by the insurgency of the legislative branch.

Because confrontation makes interesting reading and listening, Congress, in the late 1970s, was "rediscovered" by political observers, journalists, and the academic community. Thus, in recent years the federal legislature's role in the foreign-policy process has been the focus of several excellent publications. Much of that literature dwells on the conflict between the president and Congress in the field of international relations and seeks to ascertain how a more cooperative, less contentious relationship between the two branches could be established. In this study, while some redundancy is necessary to provide a background, I try to avoid duplicating the fine scholarly works already published.

Rather, as a representative who had to run for office every two years, I had ample opportunity to observe the workings of the peculiar triangular relationships between House procedures, committee and floor votes, and electoral concerns which are so significant in the legislating of our foreign policy. Moreover, since my retirement in 1979 from the House of Representatives, I have been able to return to an earlier career and teach several graduate courses on Congress and foreign policy, as well as address audiences both in the United States and abroad about different aspects of this subject. My experiences in the House and my reflections on them have led me to conclude that there is something greatly amiss in the way Congress disposes of its responsibilities in foreign policy. It is this hypothesis which I address in this book.

By 1970 House members had drastically changed their attitudes toward procedures and prerogatives that had previously gone unquestioned. Exasperated by an unpopular and seemingly aimless military commitment in Southeast Asia, frustrated by bureaucratic secrecy, and embittered by disclosures of presidential duplicity, many representatives were anxious to divorce themselves from the executive branch's conduct of international affairs and from their House leaders, who, for so long, had endorsed administration foreign policy.

Under pre-1971 procedures, however, any attempt by members to reshape foreign policy was a difficult, if not impossible, undertaking. The House literally operated behind "closed doors." Archaic rules enabled committee chairmen, who owed their positions to the seniority system, to dominate the flow of legislation. Furthermore, the prohibition on recorded votes on floor amendments greatly handicapped those who would have had the chamber embark upon an independent course in the making of foreign policy.

However, while strengthening the House's role in the foreign-policy dialogue, the reforms of the 1970s have also contributed to results that are inimical to our international interests. Post-1970 procedural changes have decentralized legislative authority and exposed members to greater public visibility, thereby enfeebling the influence of House leaders and diminishing the effectiveness of administration representatives, and created an unintended electoral problem by requiring members to take public positions on controversial questions that previously were not a matter of record. Consequently, fear of reprisal at the polls has become a concern for many representatives in determining how they will vote on foreign-policy (as well as domestic) issues; foreign-policy votes often reflect attempts by House members to minimize the potential for such damage with the electorate.

These are subjective judgments which may not lend themselves to the kind of quantitative analyses of which political scientists are so fond, but that risk is worth taking. Congress's mission is to meet our country's domestic and international needs. *How* Congress performs this task, as measured by the *quality* of its output, is a topic worthy of pursuit. But this policy product is formulated by individuals who ultimately are accountable not to the institution in which they serve but to their constituents who send them there. Thus, it is also important to know *why* legislators, in shaping foreign policy, vote and act as they do.

Two other caveats. First, my research is confined to the House of Representatives. Although I served in the Congress for twelve years, my direct observation of the Senate and its practices was necessarily limited. Second, because of my committee assignments foreign policy consumed most of my legislative attention. Thus, in this book I will deal principally with international concerns, although an analysis of the impact of the reforms on the House's disposition of domestic issues would undoubtedly develop conclusions similar to those that I reach concerning their effect on foreign policy.

CHAPTER 2

Shared Constitutional Prerogatives

A cursory reading of the Constitution confirms the conclusion of the Special Subcommittee on Investigation of the House Committee on Foreign Affairs* that this document "provides that foreign powers are shared by both the President and the Congress."[1]

Article 1, Section 8, confers upon the Congress the authority to lay and collect taxes, duties, and imposts; provide for the common defense; regulate commerce with foreign nations; coin money; declare war; raise and support armies; provide and maintain a navy; make rules for the regulation of the land and naval forces; and provide for the calling forth of the state militias to repel invasions.

Article 1, Section 9, accords the legislative branch its most potent weapon, the "power of the purse"—"No money shall be drawn from the Treasury, but in Consequence of Appropriations made by Law." Article 1, Section 7, does offer protection to the president against congressional excesses by permitting him to return bills "with his Objections [veto]" to the house of origin. Such legislation, however, can be reconsidered and enacted into law by a two-thirds affirmative vote of each body.

Article 2, which deals with the executive, enumerates only four presidential powers in the realm of international relations. Section 2 states that the president shall be commander in chief of the army and navy and the militia when called into actual service of the country. It further empowers him to make treaties and appoint ambas-

*For 186 years the House panel charged with handling matters affecting our country's international relations was called the Foreign Affairs Committee. In 1975 the committee voted to call itself the International Relations Committee. The original name was readopted in 1979. For consistency's sake, throughout this book I shall use the committee's original and current name, Foreign Affairs Committee.

sadors, but subject in each instance to the advice and consent of the Senate. Section 3 allows the president to receive foreign emissaries.

The Ebb and Flow of Foreign-Policy Supremacy

While the legislative and executive branches possess distinct constitutional privileges, they can rarely operate on separate tracks, for, as Ralph Huitt has suggested, their powers are "commingled."[2] Thus, most policies, whatever their source, cannot be implemented without prior congressional authorizing and funding legislation subsequently signed into law by the president. This "dualism of the American system" ensures that "both the President and the Congress will have powerful stakes in decision making at the national level."[3] This, in turn, explains why foreign-policy supremacy has been the shuttlecock of American politics, constantly being volleyed between the executive and legislative courts.

In 1884, for example, Woodrow Wilson, then a graduate student at Johns Hopkins University, mourned that "the predominant and controlling force"[4] was vested in a Congress in which "there [was] little coherency about the legislation agreed upon."[5] Yet by 1900, in the preface to the fifteenth printing of his 1884 graduate dissertation, Wilson optimistically noted that "the war with Spain has changed the lodgement and exercise of power within our federal system," thereby enlarging the executive's "opportunity for constructive statesmanship."[6]

Wilson himself dominated the foreign-policy agenda during the early years of his presidency. But he left office in 1921 frustrated and embittered by the unwillingness of the Senate to ratify the Treaty of Versailles, which embodied his cherished Covenant of the League of Nations.

During the Harding and Hoover administrations Congress recaptured its preeminence in international trade policy by reverting to its earlier practice of "placating particular constituents' demands" for protection against foreign competition.[7] The Fordney-McCumber Tariff Act of 1922 was followed by the Smoot-Hawley Act of 1930, which established the highest import duties in United States history. Since rates were fixed by law, the executive branch's role was restricted to the collection of customs duties.

The Depression of the 1930s, however, altered many of America's long-held economic attitudes. This enabled Franklin D. Roosevelt's secretary of state, Cordell Hull, to persuade Congress to adopt the Reciprocal Trade Agreements Act of 1934. This was "landmark legislation," noted Stephen D. Cohen, for it "represented the first transfer of tariff-setting authority from the legislative to the executive branch" by permitting the president to engage in negotiations aimed at achieving mutual reductions in trade barriers.[8]

During his first two terms, nevertheless, President Roosevelt was not always successful in gaining acceptance of his global goals. In 1935 an increasingly isolationist Congress strapped him with the Neutrality Act. Six years later, with war raging in Europe, he came within one vote (203–202) of losing his bid in the House of Representatives to extend the military draft law. (The late Speaker John McCormack was always fond of reminding us that it was *his* vote "back in 1941" that saved the Selective Service Act.)

The Japanese bombing of Pearl Harbor on December 7, 1941, radically altered relationships between the executive and legislative branches on matters of foreign policy for the next three decades. Following its declarations of war against Japan, Germany, and Italy, Congress accorded the president extensive emergency powers, including the authority to establish wage and price controls, impose food and commodity rationing, and allocate human and industrial resources. On July 28, 1945, just nine days before the United States dropped the atomic bomb on Hiroshima, the Senate, reflecting the country's determination to avoid future conflicts, ratified the United Nations Charter by an 89–2 vote. On July 31, 1945, President Harry S. Truman signed HR 3314, the Bretton Woods Arrangement Act, which committed us to membership in two other newly formed worldwide institutions, the International Bank for Reconstruction and Development (World Bank) and the International Monetary Fund (IMF).

However, following the cessation of hostilities with Germany and Japan, Congress allowed its foreign-policy powers to atrophy for another twenty-five years. Perhaps the most cogent explanation for this congressional retrenchment was offered by Senator J. William Fulbright (D.-Ark.), chairman of the Senate Foreign Relations Committee, in a statement presented on July 19, 1967, to the Subcommittee on Separation of Powers of the Senate Committee on the Judiciary: "It has been circumstances rather than design which has given the Executive its great predominance in foreign policy. The circumstance has been crises, an entire era of crises in which urgent decisions of a kind that the Congress is ill-equipped to make with what was thought to be the requisite speed. The President has the means at his disposal for prompt action, the Congress does not."[9]

The foundation for each of these "crises" was the same: adoption by our government (after Russia's failure to liberate those lands that its troops had occupied on their march to Germany in 1944–45) of a bipartisan determination to contain Communist expansionism in both Europe and Asia. This resulted, in May 1947, in overwhelming congressional acceptance of the "Truman Doctrine" (PL 80-75), a $400-million aid package designed to support the efforts of Greece and Turkey to resist "attempted subjugation by armed minorities [and] outside pressure."[10] On April 3, 1948, President Truman signed S 2202, thereby implementing the European Recovery Program (Marshall Plan) which, between 1948 and 1951, provided that continent with $11.85 billion in economic assistance plus an additional $1.2 billion in direct military support.

Economic assistance represented only one plank in President Truman's platform to protect the free nations of Europe "against internal and external aggression."[11] After lengthy negotiations the United States and its European allies agreed on April 4, 1949, to establish the North Atlantic Treaty Organization (NATO). Article 5 of that treaty declares that an attack against one member country will be deemed an attack against all. After ten days of often noisy and acrimonious debate, fostered largely by the clause that rejected our first president's advice concerning "entangling alliances," senators gave their "advice and consent" on July 20, 1949, to the NATO treaty by an 82–13 margin.

Initially, our country's containment plans required legislative concurrence. However, later actions justified by the policy of containment included a series of presidential military adventures undertaken without congressional assent. During the period July 12, 1948–May 12, 1949, for example, President Truman ordered over 250,000 flights over communist-occupied territory to break the Soviet blockade of West Berlin. On June 27, 1950, responding to a request from the United Nations Security Council, Truman directed that United States air and sea forces "give the Korean Government troops cover and support" in their defense against invading North

Korean armies.[12] Thus began a military commitment which ultimately cost 33,600 American lives on the battlefield. To preserve the tenuous 1953 truce with North Korea and the People's Republic of China our government still had 39,975 troops stationed in South Korea at the end of 1980.[13]

In April 1957, Truman's successor, Dwight D. Eisenhower, heeding a plea for help from Jordan's King Hussein, moved the Sixth Fleet from the French Riviera to the eastern Mediterranean to intimidate communist-organized rioters in Amman. On July 15, 1958, Eisenhower dispatched to Lebanon the first of fourteen thousand American soldiers to thwart a threatened coup d'état. During this 102-day operation one serviceman was killed and the monetary cost to the United States was $200 million.[14]

During the 1960s Southeast Asia and Latin America became the focal points of presidential containment efforts. On April 14, 1961, President John F. Kennedy gave the "green light" to a secret plan formulated by the outgoing Eisenhower administration for an invasion of Cuba by twenty-five hundred émigrés from that country. That mission ended in failure when the Cuban Brigade, trained and equipped by the Central Intelligence Agency (CIA), was destroyed by Castro's forces a few hours after its landing at Playa Giron on the Bay of Pigs. Eighteen months later, President Kennedy revealed his decision to impose a naval blockade on Cuba to halt further Soviet buildup of a nuclear strike capacity on that island. This time Kennedy prevailed. He was informed in October 1962 by Nikita Khrushchev, first secretary of Russia's Communist party, that the Soviets would dismantle and withdraw the missiles that they had recently installed in Cuba.

On April 28, 1965, President Lyndon B. Johnson had deployed four hundred marines to the Dominican Republic to prevent, as he later described it, "a well-trained, disciplined band of communists" from destroying that country.[15] By the time the last United States serviceman left that island on September 21, 1966, as Johnson put it, nineteen "of our own American boys lost their lives."[16]

However, it was the undeclared war in Indochina which finally toppled the "imperial presidency." The United States first became involved in the Vietnam civil war in May 1950 when President Truman approved the funding of French military efforts to defeat Ho Chi Minh's drive for independence in that country. Despite that assistance, French troops remained on the defensive, finally surren-

dering to General Giap at Dien Bien Phu on May 7, 1954. The ensuing Geneva accord, concluded on July 21, 1954, provided for a
cease-fire and a temporary division of Vietnam at the 17th parallel.
It also permitted the United States to send seven hundred advisers
to train South Vietnam's army, an option which President Eisenhower soon utilized. John Kennedy gradually increased that number, and by the time of his death in November 1963 seventeen
thousand American service personnel were in South Vietnam.

On August 4, 1964, possibly reacting to violations of their own
territory, the North Vietnamese attacked two American destroyers,
the *Maddox* and the *C. Turner Joy*, in the Gulf of Tonkin. While
both ships escaped unscathed, that incident presented President
Johnson with the opportunity to submit to Congress, on August 5, a
resolution which his staff had composed three months earlier. With
only two negative votes,* Congress quickly adopted this joint resolution which called for the president "to promote the maintenance
of international peace in Southeast Asia." As President Johnson told
me on August 17, 1967, he considered this action equivalent to a
declaration of war and said that "Congress certainly was aware of
that."[17] However legislators may have viewed the meaning of the
Gulf of Tonkin Resolution, its passage immersed the United States in
a bloody war from which we were unable to extricate ourselves for
another nine years and five days.

The troubled 1960s ended with the United States still mired in
Southeast Asia. In the sixty-five months since Lyndon Johnson had
employed the Gulf of Tonkin Resolution to expand our presence in
South Vietnam, 39,914 GIs had been killed in action.† Our nation
was deeply divided. On "Vietnam Moratorium Day," October 15,
1969, one hundred thousand citizens gathered in Boston and another one hundred thousand gathered in New York City to protest
the war. In mid-November 1969 two hundred and fifty thousand
people participated in a "March against Death" in Washington. Student unrest and violence permeated American college campuses. In
the face of this turmoil, President Richard M. Nixon (who succeeded
Johnson in 1969), using the familiar pretext of protecting "our

---

*Senators Wayne Morse (D.-Ore.) and Ernest Gruening (D.-Alaska).
†Another 7,164 servicemen had died from other causes. According to Department of
Defense figures, by the end of the war in 1973, 47,072 Americans had lost their lives
in battle and another 10,435 had died from nonhostile causes.

men,"[18] on April 30, 1970, directed American and South Vietnamese ground forces to attack Vietcong sanctuaries in Cambodia. This widening of the conflict not only galvanized further domestic opposition to the war but also awakened Congress from a twenty-five year slumber.

Members' Changing Attitudes

Speaker Sam Rayburn's oft-quoted first words of advice to incoming freshmen members were: "To get along, go along." Rayburn continued his orientation lecture by reminding the newcomers, "You must please the people of your district. And if you want to be in a position which will enable you to help and please these people, you must also please your colleagues in the House. . . . That does not imply that anybody has to become a rubber stamp. . . . But when there is an umpire in the game and a rule is made, I learned in baseball that it's a poor player who becomes angry, throws his bat at an umpire and quits the game like a spoiled child."

On occasion Rayburn gave specific suggestions to individuals who inquired how they might become more effective in the House. To one new representative who asked if Rayburn thought he was talking too much, the speaker grunted yes. "What should I do about it?" queried the member. "Quit it," Rayburn replied. When first-termer Adam Clayton Powell (D.-N.Y.) solicited his counsel, Mr. Sam told the controversial Harlem minister: "Everybody thinks you're coming down here with a bomb in each hand. Maybe you are. But don't throw them. Feel your way around. You have a great future."[19]

By the end of the 1960s, however, many House members were no longer "going along" or "feeling their way around." Conduct that would have brought isolation on the offending member a decade earlier suddenly became tolerable if not laudable in 1970. Angered by an accumulation of grievances, a substantial number of representatives were ready to cut the House's foreign-policy ties (which had endured for twenty-nine years) with the executive branch and challenge their House leaders and committee elders. Freshmen no longer were being "seen but not heard." Mid-ranking congressmen were demanding legislative powers heretofore denied them. Beginning in 1970, the House began to make changes in long-cherished norms, to divorce itself from the executive's conduct of international affairs, and, simultaneously, to revise its own operating processes.

Reassertion in Foreign Policy

In their *Foreign Affairs* article "Making the Separation of Powers Work," Representative Lee H. Hamilton and Foreign Affairs Committee staff counsel Michael Van Dusen conceded that many factors contributed to Congress's reassertiveness in foreign policy. "But to any member whose service goes back to 1965 [Hamilton was first elected in 1964], there is no question that Vietnam was the single most important event in the transformation."[20] As former Senate Foreign Relations Committee chairman John Sparkman (D.-Ala.) explained, "Vietnam became the catalyst for an extended self-examination by Congress as to its own proper role in the making of foreign policy and for the subsequent reaffirmation of long-neglected checks and balances."[21]

This institutional self-analysis was made all the more urgent by the growing congressional mistrust of the executive. Bluntly stated, many legislators no longer could believe the president and his staff.

The Gulf of Tonkin Resolution was a case in point. The *Pentagon Papers* disclosed that for six months prior to the Gulf of Tonkin incidents in August 1964 "the United States had been mounting clandestine military attacks against North Vietnam." Designated "Operation 34A," these efforts "ranged from flights over North Vietnam by U-2 spy planes and kidnapping of North Vietnam citizens for intelligence information, to parachuting sabotage and psychological-warfare teams into the North, commando raids from the sea to blow-up rail and highway bridges, and the bombardment of North Vietnamese coastal installations by PT boats."[22] Advanced monthly plans were submitted by Saigon headquarters to Washington for approval. Secretary of Defense Robert S. McNamara and Secretary of State Dean Rusk were regularly informed of the planned and conducted raids.

However, during the Senate Foreign Relations Committee's hearing on the Gulf of Tonkin Resolution, McNamara and Rusk had both professed to have no knowledge of those and other military actions planned and directed by the United States against North Vietnam. The record, when finally made public, clearly indicated otherwise.

This pattern of deceit was perpetuated by the Nixon administration. Congress learned only many months afterward that in 1969 secret B-52 bombing missions had been carried out over Cambodia.

Later, of course, self-survival prompted the withholding of facts related to the Watergate affair. I shall never forget a coffee meeting with H. R. Haldeman in the spring of 1973. With a disarming grin, the assistant to the president assured several of my colleagues and me that he had never heard of a secret campaign fund before reading about it in the *Washington Post* (the story first surfaced in the October 25, 1972, edition). Clearly, if it was to gain access to information bearing upon foreign-policy decisions, Congress could no longer remain supine.

Inadvertently, the Vietnam War provided still another part of the explanation for congressional foreign-policy activism. Following the 1970, 1972, and 1974 elections, a total of 201 representatives (120 Democrats and 81 Republicans) took their seats in Congress for the first time. During the Ninety-fourth Congress (1975–76) 43.4 percent of the House's members (122 Democrats and 76 Republicans) had served three terms or less. Many of those newcomers had made the Vietnam War their principal campaign issue. One of these was Andrew Young (D.-Ga.), who was later appointed our permanent representative to the United Nations. In his maiden speech to the United Nations General Assembly, Young related how, during his first congressional contest in 1972, he had made the centerpiece of his campaign the "end-the-war" amendment that Lucien N. Nedzi and I had sponsored the previous year.*

---

*On June 17, 1971, Congressman Lucien N. Nedzi (D.-Mich.) and I obtained the first recorded vote in the House on the Vietnam War. Those who entitled it the "Nedzi-Whalen End the War Amendment" could have been accused of misleading advertising, for the amendment's language would not have extricated us from Indochina. Nevertheless, it would have precluded the use in Southeast Asia of any equipment authorized by the Fiscal Year 1973 Military Procurement Bill (HR 8687), to which we sought to append the amendment. Common Cause, a citizens' "public interest" lobby headed by former HEW secretary John Gardner, circulated the language of the amendment among its members, who promptly deluged the House with mail urging its passage. Despite this outpouring of constituent communications the Nedzi-Whalen amendment was defeated 158–254.

So it was inevitable that Young and others who had been elected on a foreign-policy platform and lacked any memory of or respect for the previously honored "to get along, go along" mores would continue their active involvement in that subject upon arriving in Washington.

By 1973 Congress found it easier to join the foreign-policy fray as the evidence of a weakened presidency became unmistakably clear. After an overwhelming reelection victory on November 7, 1972 (when he received 61.8 percent of the popular vote and carried forty-nine of fifty states), Nixon suffered a precipitous drop in public support during 1973. His approval rating in the Gallup Poll, which stood at 63 percent on March 8, dwindled steadily to 40 percent on July 22, 31 percent on August 15, and 27 percent on November 4.[23] This descent reflected the citizenry's uneasiness about our continued conduct of military operations in Southeast Asia and the unfolding Watergate drama.

On January 12–15, 1973, the Gallup organization took a poll on the question "Do you think the United States made a mistake in sending troops to fight in Vietnam?" According to the published results 60 percent replied yes, 29 percent answered no, and 11 percent offered no opinion.[24] This contrasted sharply with the January 31, 1965, Gallup survey, which found that 50 percent of the American people supported the use of our military forces in Southeast Asia, only 28 percent were opposed, and 22 percent had no opinion.[25] As the war drew to a close, even our last-ditch bombing of Communist bases in Cambodia and Laos was disapproved by 57 percent of those responding to a Gallup Poll conducted on April 27–30, 1973.[26] By then on the wrong side of an unpopular issue, President Nixon was easy prey for a congressional "second guess."

June 17, 1972, marked the beginning of our nation's greatest political scandal. That evening Washington police apprehended five men in the process of ransacking the Democratic National Committee's headquarters located in the Watergate office-apartment complex. During his race that fall against President Nixon, Senator George McGovern attempted to capitalize on the break-in, but it ignited little voter reaction.

However, on March 23, 1973, following his conviction, one of the five conspirators, James W. McCord, Jr., informed presiding judge John J. Sirica that perjury had been committed during the trial and that the defendants had been under considerable pressure to plead guilty so as to foreclose any further pursuit of the case. In his letter to Judge Sirica, McCord also implicated in the plot three senior White House officials, former attorney general John N. Mitchell, presidential legal counsel John W. Dean III, and Jeb Magruder, an officer of the Committee to Reelect the President. The ensuing investigations by the media, the reconvened federal grand jury, and the Senate Select Committee chaired by Sam Ervin (D.-N.C.) brought the crime closer to the Oval Office. To dampen growing criticism, President Nixon on May 18, 1973, affirmed the selection by newly appointed attorney general Elliot Richardson of Harvard Law professor Archibald Cox to head an independent investigation of the events surrounding the Watergate burglary attempt.

Five months later, when Cox refused to forego further plans to obtain evidence through court-enforced subpoenas of presidential tapes and papers, Nixon ordered Richardson to discharge the special investigator. Rather than obey this directive, the attorney general resigned, as did his deputy, William Ruckelshaus. The Cox sacking was finally effected by Acting Attorney General Robert H. Bork. To students of history those bizarre events of October 20, 1973, will forever be known as the "Saturday night massacre."

With each new revelation the clamor for Nixon's impeachment mounted. The percentage of Gallup Poll interviewees favoring removal of the president grew from 18 percent on July 8 to 37 percent on November 13, 1973, to 48 percent on May 27, 1974, and, finally, to 57 percent on August 7, 1974.[27]

The national nightmare abruptly ended on August 9, 1974, with Nixon's resignation. During the sixteen months between James McCord's confession and Nixon's departure for San Clemente, Congress had ample opportunity to fill a power vacuum created by the president's all-consuming preoccupation with Watergate.

A Democratic-controlled Congress could suffer no embarrassment by inflicting further injury on an already wounded president of the other party. In fact, looking toward 1976, it made good political sense for the majority party to pursue legislative tactics that kept President Nixon and his successor, Gerald Ford, on the defensive. A good illustration of this tack in the foreign-policy area was the War Powers Resolution of 1973. This proposal, which curbs the ability of the president to commit troops to military action, was vetoed by Nixon on October 24, 1973. Twelve Democrats, who opposed both the House resolution and the conference report, voted to override the veto. Had they maintained their original position—several were concerned that the resolution substantially broadened, rather than reduced, the president's war-making authority—the veto would have been sustained by a 272–147 margin. Instead, Nixon emerged the loser in his battle with the Democrats to block legislation that had widespread public support (a November 18, 1973, Gallup Poll showed 80 percent in favor of requiring the president to secure congressional approval before sending United States armed forces into action outside our borders).[28]

Procedural Reform

The convergence of all of the foregoing elements presented a solid case for a more direct congressional role in America's foreign-policy dialogue. But ability is not always consonant with desire. As will be detailed in the next chapter, House procedures in 1970 made it extremely difficult for members to be responsive to the concerns of a disaffected society. Therefore, those representatives who wished to reassert Congress's foreign-policy prerogatives, had first to change the "rules of the game."*

It is axiomatic that those who wield power have a vested interest in the status quo. It remained, therefore, for the rank and file, rather than the House leadership and committee chairmen, to activate the reform movement of the 1970s. As Norman J. Ornstein noted in his analysis of the causes and consequences of congressional change, the legislative reforms of the 1970s emanated from those "short-changed of power" who were seeking a "payoff."[29] Payoff represented different things to different individuals and factions.

For liberal Democrats it meant overcoming such institutional disadvantages as domination of House committees by a large number of elderly (average age, 68.1 years in 1970), relatively conservative chairmen, a dependence upon the committee for information relating to pending legislation, and a prohibition against recorded votes on amendments offered during floor debate. As early as September 1959, Democrat liberals had organized to combat these bar-

*The last major House uprising occurred in 1910 when Speaker Joseph G. Cannon, an Illinois Republican, was shorn of his almost monarchical authority.

riers, when they formed the Democratic Study Group (DSG). Procedural change, while a major DSG aim, was not viewed as a goal per se. Rather, it was considered a medium by which the House of Representatives "could translate the Democratic platform into legislative action."[30]

For House Republicans, including the party leadership, the payoff for reform was that it offered a more progressive image, greater protection of rights of the congressional minority, and an increase in the number of staff slots. But most importantly (at least until 1969), Republicans viewed a "modernized Congress" as "an essential check on the massive power of the Executive"![31]

On January 24, 1963, Gerald Ford, then chairman of the House Republican Conference (the equivalent of the Democratic Caucus), had appointed Representative Fred Schwengel of Iowa to head a Subcommittee on Minority Staffing. Although the Schwengel group failed to secure budget approval for the thirty new staff positions that it sought in 1963, the mood for reform did not die within the GOP's ranks. After Schwengel's defeat in the 1964 election, he was succeeded as task force chairman by James C. Cleveland of New Hampshire. In 1965, Cleveland and twenty-one Republican colleagues published a book, *We Propose to Modernize Congress*, which provided the impetus for minority-party support of later reform efforts.

Finally, for junior House members, procedural revamping offered the opportunity to acquire greater legislative responsibilities. It provided them the chance to construct a leadership bus with more seats.

Pre-1970 House reformers had found an ally in Senator Joseph S. Clark (D.-Pa.), who had a long-standing disagreement with the method by which his fellow Democrats were assigned to Senate committees. They had combined forces in 1965 to secure congressional approval of a Joint Committee on the Organization of Congress. Most of the Joint Committee's recommendations, filed in 1966, were incorporated in a bill, S 355, which passed the Senate on March 7, 1967. However, S 355 died at the end of the Ninetieth Congress when House Rules Committee Chairman William S. Colmer (D.-Miss.), with the tacit concurrence of Speaker John W. McCormack (D.-Mass.), refused to bring it to a vote in his committee.

When the Ninety-first Congress convened in the Capitol on January 3, 1969, the reformers of the early 1960s were augmented by anti–Vietnam War members of both parties who saw procedural change as the only means of obtaining a vote on the war. Yielding to this increased pressure, Chairman Colmer in April named Representative B. F. Sisk (D.-Cal.) to chair a special five-member subcommittee of the House Rules Committee to consider proposals dealing with legislative reorganization. The Sisk panel's product, HR 17654, the Legislative Reorganization Act of 1970, was adopted on June 17, 1970, by the full committee. After accepting thirty-six floor amendments, the House approved HR 17654 on September 17 by a vote of 326–19. On October 6 the Senate passed HR 17654, retaining all of the House provisions except those which directly related to the operations of "the other body" (as the Senate is referred to by House members). The Legislative Reorganization Act of 1970 was sent to President Nixon for his signature on October 8 when the House, by voice vote, agreed to accept the Senate's amendments. HR 17654 only partially assuaged House reformers. But it did represent a significant step toward opening the doors of the House of Representatives to public scrutiny, as well as reducing the control of committee proceedings by arbitrary chairmen.

For several years following passage of that act the House Democratic Caucus served as the battleground for further reform. The caucus, which includes all Democratic members of the House of Representatives, meets periodically to discuss party business, including legislative policy and strategy, committee appointments, and other matters relating to the operation of the House. It is guided by the standing rules adopted by its members and by a manual which contains all resolutions of continuing force and effect.

In a Special Report issued November 6, 1978, the DSG called the caucus the "key to the reform movement." According to the DSG, "following the era of 'King Caucus' from 1910 to 1920, the Caucus gradually fell into disuse and the seniority system took hold. Thus, during the 1950s and 1960s the Caucus met only for a brief pro forma session at the beginning of each Congress to elect the Democratic leadership and other House officers and to pass a resolution designating the Democratic members of the Ways and Means Committee as the Committee on Committees." With the support of Majority Leader Carl Albert, the DSG, in January 1969, won approval of rules changes "requiring monthly meetings of the Caucus [and] giving individual Members the right to bring matters before the Caucus for debate and action. . . . These changes were fundamental for they permitted use of the Caucus to win many of the other reforms."[32]

Many of these other reforms were proposals suggested by a special committee chaired by Congresswoman Julia Butler Hansen (D.-Wash.). First established by the caucus on March 18, 1970, as a consolation to liberal Democrats who a year earlier had failed to unseat Speaker McCormack, the Hansen Committee was commissioned to study the tendentious seniority question. After adopting the first set of Hansen recommendations on January 30, 1971, the caucus extended the committee's life and directed it to consider further procedural changes for submission to the Ninety-third Congress (1973–74). The proposed revisions resulting from the second Hansen study were affirmed by the caucus on January 23, 1973. Representative Hansen's special committee was reactivated on May 9, 1974, to develop jurisdictional and structural reforms acceptable to the caucus, which, that same day, had rejected plans drafted by a bipartisan select committee created by the House on January 31, 1973. Eleven weeks later the caucus approved the Hansen group's outline for committee realignment, one less ambitious in its scope than that detailed earlier by the House select committee.

The Legislative Reorganization Act of 1970 and the edicts of the Democratic Caucus dealt only with the internal operating rules of the House of Representatives. They did not address the procedures governing relationships between the executive and legislative branches. This meant that existing law had to be amended by statutory enactment before Congress could develop a more independent policy role vis-à-vis the President. Congress, therefore, passed legislation during the 1970s that enhanced its information and research capabilities; defined responsibilities of the commander in chief and the legislative branch in situations where American troops are exposed to actual or imminent hostilities; provided legislators with a more coherent approach to fiscal policy; imposed limits on government-to-government arms sales; and restricted the ability of the CIA to engage in covert operations abroad.

Conclusion

It was no coincidence that procedural changes and the reentrance of the House into the foreign-policy arena proceeded along parallel tracks. Both began with the radicalization of the attitudes of members as a result of frustration with the leadership, the executive, and the restrictive code within which the House conducted its business. Rule reform, therefore, became the means; policy redirection, the end. The following chapters outline the scope of these reforms and analyze their effect upon institutional practices, foreign-policy performance, and electoral consequences.

CHAPTER 3

The "New" House

House rules were not changed overnight. Instead, most procedural revisions were adopted in piecemeal fashion between 1970 and 1974. But if the reforms were approved bit by bit, their sponsors followed throughout the period a consistent formula aimed at achieving three distinct, but mutually reinforcing, aims: decentralization of power within the House; greater openness in House procedures; and strengthened House capacity to deal with the executive branch.

Decentralization of Power within the House

Committee Appointments

In 1911 the Democratic members of the Ways and Means Committee inherited the duty of apportioning House committee seats among their party colleagues. This eventually led to two problems. First, committee appointments were made by an independent group operating outside the leadership structure. Second, during most of the intervening years conservatives were over-represented on the tax-writing committee. As late as 1969 six of the Ways and Means Committee's fifteen Democrats, including the chairman, were southern conservatives. Understandably, liberal Democrats were disturbed by this regional imbalance, which they believed impeded their ability to bargain for choice committee positions.

In December 1974–January 1975, emboldened by Chairman Wilbur Mills's (D.-Ark.) highly publicized personal problems,* liberals forced a caucus vote that stripped the Ways and Means Committee of its appointive power. In a move designed to strengthen the party's leadership the caucus transferred to the speaker the right to name Democrats to the Rules Committee, subject to caucus affirmation. Responsibility for assigning Democrats to the other standing committees was shifted to the Steering and Policy Committee which, in its Committee on Committees capacity, "shall make recommendations to the Caucus regarding the assignment of members to each committee other than the Committee on Rules, one committee at a time. Upon demand supported by 10% or more members, a separate [caucus] vote shall be had on any member of the Committee."[1] This process, incidentally, parallels the appointive method employed for many years by House Republicans.

Section M1. E of the caucus manual also guarantees each Democrat an important committee assignment by limiting Democratic representatives to membership on only two committees each, one "exclusive" or "major" committee and one "nonmajor" committee. The House's three most sought-after committees—Appropriations, Ways and Means, and Rules—are deemed "exclusive." "Major" committees include Agriculture, Armed Services, Banking, Finance and Urban Affairs, Education and Labor, Foreign Affairs, Interstate and Foreign Commerce, Public Works, and Transportation. Defined as "nonmajor" are the Budget, District of Columbia, Government Operations, House Administration, Interior and Insular Affairs, Merchant Marine and Fisheries, Post Office and Civil Service, Science and Technology, Small Business, and Veterans Affairs committees.

Committee Chairmen

The so-called seniority system, stated Congressman Richard Bolling (D.-Mo.), "has no constitutional sanction, . . . is not a law, [and] is not a rule of the House."[2] Yet for almost a century it determined the selection of House committee leaders by specifying that "a member first named to a committee shall be its chairman."[3]

---

*Mills was involved in several bizarre episodes which made headlines in 1974. He finally underwent treatment for alcoholism, an illness which he eventually overcame.

One reason for the persistence of this method of selecting committee chairmen for so many years was given by Lewis A. Froman, Jr., in his book *The Congressional Process—Strategies, Rules and Procedures*: "The Seniority rule . . . is a useful device whereby a party with many factions can avoid the inevitable fights over at least some leadership positions."[4] By 1970, however, sensing it had sufficient votes in the Democratic Caucus, the liberal faction stood ready to upset this tradition of "respect your elders."

Procedural revisions inaugurated during the period 1970–75 modified but did not entirely abolish the seniority principle. Years of service on a committee remain a starting point for the caucus's Steering and Policy Committee. In 1975, 1977, 1979, and 1981, with only two exceptions,* senior members of each of the House's standing committees were recommended by the Steering and Policy Committee to head their panels.

By 1975 the caucus rules had been amended to require an automatic secret vote on each person proposed by the Steering and Policy Committee for a committee chairmanship. If the selectee chaired the committee during the preceding session of Congress or is the surviving senior member, no other nomination is in order. The caucus then votes yes or no. But if the Steering and Policy Committee does not follow seniority as the basis for its selection, "additional nominations are in order from the floor of the Caucus."

Section M1. D of the caucus manual mandates that if the initial choice is rejected, the Steering and Policy Committee "shall make a new nomination within 5 days," and 5 to 10 days thereafter "the Caucus shall meet to consider the new nominee . . . and any additional nominations from the Floor."[5]

Subcommittee Chairmen

Before 1971 seniority not only dictated the selection of committee leaders but was also determinant in the process by which subcommittee chairmen were named. Starting with the committee chair-

---

*Representatives Wright Patman (Tex.) and Wayne L. Hays (Ohio), chairmen, respectively, during the Ninety-third Congress of the Banking and Currency Committee and the House Administration Committee, were passed over by the Steering and Policy Committee in 1975. The caucus sustained the Patman rejection, but overruled the Steering and Policy Committee by voting to rename Hays as chairman of the House Administration Committee for the Ninety-fourth Congress.

man, subcommittee chairs were filled in order of members' service on the committee. This system obviously favored veteran representatives, many of whom had lengthy tenure on two or more committees. Consequently, in 1969 twenty-five House Democrats were able to claim two subcommittee chairs; an additional five headed three subcommittees; one member, F. Edward Hebert (La.), wielded the gavel in four subcommittees.

This ability of party elders to secure multiple subcommittee chairmanships ended in 1971. Early that year the Democratic Caucus approved section M2. B of the manual, which stated, "No Member shall be chairman of more than one subcommittee of a committee with legislative jurisdiction."[6]* The right of Democratic members "to bid, in order of full committee seniority, for subcommittee chairmanship on that committee"[7] was retained by the caucus. However, with this "one-per-customer" limitation, many high-ranking Democrats now must decide among several available chairs.

Once a member opts for a subcommittee chairmanship, section M5. A of the caucus manual subjects the bidder to the "approval by a majority of those present and voting by secret ballot at the Democratic Caucus of the committee." This section also stipulates that "the full Democratic Caucus . . . shall vote on each Member nominated to serve as chairman of an Appropriations subcommittee."[8]

After clearing the caucus hurdle the subcommittee chairman is then entitled "to select and designate at least one staff member for said subcommittee, subject to the approval of a majority of the Democratic Members of said full committee."[9]

Subcommittee Rights

In the prereform era many committee chairman considered subcommittees as their private domains. Often they created or disbanded subcommittees without consulting committee colleagues. Granting or withholding subcommittee assignments was a common means of rewarding loyalists and punishing miscreants. Frequently, committee chairmen limited subcommittee functions to investigation, oversight, and nominal legislative jurisdiction. What legislative prerogatives the subcommittee did possess could be

---

*In 1977 the caucus extended the rule to cover nonlegislative subcommittees as well.

negated by a committee chairman's decision to lock in his desk drawer for the duration of the session bills that were antithetical to his beliefs.

The twenty committee chiefs were eventually overwhelmed in the Democratic Caucus by their juniors' demands for subcommittee reform. The caucus agreed to direct all committees with twenty or more members to create at least four subcommittees. Also accepted was a motion that "there shall be a Democratic Caucus of each standing committee," which is empowered to "establish the number of subcommittees, . . . fix the jurisdiction of each subcommittee, and . . . determine the size of each subcommittee."[10]

To spread the choice assignments, the new caucus rules limited Democrats to service on no more than five subcommittees and protected new committee members by allowing them to "choose any one subcommittee assignment to the extent that subcommittee size permits."[11]

The caucus manual orders a committee chairman to refer all bills and other matters to subcommittees of appropriate jurisdiction within two weeks of receipt unless a majority of the Democratic members votes for full committee consideration. Each subcommittee is also assured of a sufficient staff and budget "to discharge its responsibilities for legislation and oversight."[12]

Greater Openness in House Procedures

Committee and Subcommittee Proceedings

Prior to 1970 House committee activities could best be described as shrouded in secrecy. According to the *Congressional Quarterly Almanac*, spectators were barred from 48 percent of committee and subcommittee sessions held in 1970.[13] Records of the votes cast by committee members during these closed meetings were unavailable to the press and other interested parties. There were no written guidelines pertaining to the scheduling of meetings, the calling of witnesses, or the filing of committee reports.

In separate floor actions in 1970 and 1973 the House directed that all full and subcommittee hearings, other than those dealing with national security matters or involving discussions of personal character, be open to the public. Other meetings can be closed only by a majority vote of the committee or subcommittee. Such a decision may be made either in advance of the session or at the time that the members assemble for the meeting. House panels are now permitted to invite federal officials to attend closed sessions to provide bill-drafting assistance.

The cloak of anonymity was removed from committee members when the House ordained that all roll calls be published and that the tally on final passage be incorporated in the reports accompanying all committee bills. Other important committee-related reforms adopted by the House of Representatives during the last decade included: the right of the speaker to refer a bill to two or more committees (in split, joint, or sequential referral); the requirement that hearings be scheduled one week in advance; the permission for a majority of minority party members to call witnesses; the right to broadcast or televise committee hearings; the provision that committee reports be filed within seven legislative days if requested in writing by a majority of the members; a three-day time allowance for those who wish to insert opposing or supplementary views in the committee report.

Floor Procedures

On May 10, 1967, the House Republican Policy Committee issued a position paper calling for legislation to "update and modernize Congress." The Policy Committee maintained that "the awesome problems of today and the challenges of the 70s demand an efficient and effective Congress." The report concluded by urging adoption of "new procedures and techniques."[14]

Earlier the American Federation of Labor and Congress of Industrial Organizations (AFL-CIO), not normally a Republican ally, made a similar diagnosis. Its resolution on congressional reform adopted in the 1963 AFL-CIO convention declared: "Until congressional reformation is achieved, America will be trying to resolve its vast automation and atomic age problems with a horse-and-buggy legislative mechanism."[15]

The principal contributors to this defective mechanism were the methods by which the House of Representatives had traditionally conducted its business on the floor. As a consequence, floor operating rules became the object of many of the reforms that the House instituted during the 1970s.

The following is a summary of these modifications:

> Committees are now allowed to continue their delibera-tions while the House is in session. Unless objection is regis-tered on the floor by ten or more members, the committee may also sit during the "five-minute rule" (when floor amend-ments are being debated).
>
> After a quorum has been established in the Committee of the Whole* no further quorum calls are in order unless the body is operating under the five-minute rule and the chair-man has put the pending motion or proposition to a vote. Once one hundred members have registered their presence, the call is discontinued and no record is made of those who did or did not respond.
>
> Committee reports must be available to House members for at least three days, excluding Saturday, Sunday, and legal holidays, before the bills to which they pertain can be consid-ered on the House floor. Previously, committee chairmen

---

* When the House is ready to take up a bill, it "resolves itself into the Committee of the Whole." At this time the speaker leaves the dais and is replaced by a chairman whom he has appointed to preside over the ensuing deliberations. The Rules Com-mittee specifies the conditions which govern consideration of the measure. Usually one or more hours are allocated for general debate, with half of the time assigned to a spokesperson for the majority party and the other half of the time going to a repre-sentative of the minority party. These two individuals then dispense time increments to the members of their respective parties who wish to speak during general debate. It often happens that the proposal has the support of both the Democratic and the Republican members who control the time. Therefore, they must use prudence in dividing it between the "pro's" and "con's" within their parties.

After general debate is concluded, the bill is then open for amendment (unless a "closed rule" has been ordered by the Rules Committee, in which case no amend-ments may be offered). At this point the five-minute rule applies. This simply means that the remarks of the representative who introduces the amendment and of those who speak on its behalf or in opposition are limited to five minutes each.

Those in the gallery who are following the floor action usually cannot distinguish between proceedings conducted in the full House and those in the Committee of the Whole. The veteran House-watcher looks for the mace, which is positioned to the left (as viewed from the balcony) of the speaker's chair. If it is present, the members are sitting as the House; if removed, they are acting as the Committee of the Whole.

could bring measures to the floor without affording House members an opportunity to study them.

The "closed rule," which proscribes floor amendments, is now subject to appeal by members of the majority party. If fifty or more Democrats propose that an amendment be made in order, and a majority of the caucus concurs, the Democratic members of the Rules Committee then are instructed to write a rule allowing that specific amendment to reach the floor.

Ten minutes of debate are now guaranteed to those whose amendments are printed in the *Congressional Record* at least one day before their consideration. Before 1970, if all time had expired, amendments were voted upon without debate.

When all debate ends, the minority party, just prior to the vote on final passage, may offer a motion to recommit the pending bill "with instructions" (that is, "instructing" the House to adopt certain designated amendments that had previously been rejected in the Committee of the Whole). Instead of no debate, as formerly, ten minutes, equally divided between proponents and opponents, are allowed for a discussion of the motion.

Rather than continue the previous practice of ordering a vote upon the conclusion of debate on each bill being considered under "suspension of the rules,"* the speaker presently may accumulate the votes until the end of the day or on the following day. At that time members have fifteen minutes to respond to the first vote and five minutes for each subsequent one. This "clustering" process also may be utilized by the

---

*At least once a week (usually Monday, Tuesday, and the last six days of the session) the House considers bills that committee chairmen bring directly to the floor without first obtaining a rule from the Rules Committee. These measures, normally noncontroversial, are not open to amendment. House rule 27 stipulates that "before the final vote is taken thereon, it shall be in order to debate the proposition . . . for forty minutes, one-half of such time to be given to debate in favor of, and one-half to debate in opposition to, such proposition." At the end of the debate the House votes on the question: "Shall the rules be suspended and the House pass H.R. ____?" The rule can be suspended only when supported by "two-thirds of the members voting, a quorum being present." It is this two-thirds requirement which gives pause to chairmen who otherwise might be tempted to bring an unamendable bill to the floor.

speaker when recorded votes are demanded on Rules Committee reports.

The House also adopted several new rules governing the way in which conference reports* are handled. The speaker is required to name as conferees those who are primarily responsible for the legislation, as well as those who are the authors of the principal provisions of the bill. Every conference report must be printed as a House report and accompanied by an explanatory statement prepared jointly by House and Senate conferees. The reports also must appear in the *Congressional Record* at least three days in advance of floor action, except during the last six days of the session. Any House member, by lodging a point of order which is sustained by the speaker, is assured of a separate vote on nongermane amendments added by the Senate to a House bill. Whereas the conference chairman formerly controlled the debate, the time is now equally divided between the majority and minority parties.

During the early months of the 1977 session the House approved experimentation with television coverage of its floor proceedings. On October 27, 1977, the House paved the way for an expanded system but, in so doing, prohibited anyone but its own employees from operating the system. High-quality color cameras were installed early in 1979, and in March 1979 the public witnessed for the first time on its television screens House floor activities. *Congressional Quarterly Almanac* reported that by April 3, 1979, "cable television systems in more than 370 communities in all 50 states began carrying broadcast proceedings of the House."[16]

---

* A conference committee is composed of representatives of both the Senate and House who are appointed by their leaders to reconcile differences in a bill that has passed both chambers. On occasion, just after the selection of conferees has been announced by the speaker, a motion is offered to "instruct" the House conferees to "insist" on retention in the bill of certain House language or to "accept" as a part of the bill a particular Senate provision not appearing in the House version. If approved, the motion does not obligate the House conferees to achieve the desired objective. However, if the instructions are not carried out, the conferees have the embarrassing task of explaining to the House why its mandate was ignored. If the House still insists on its position, it can then reject the conference report and a new conference committee is created.

Recorded Floor Amendment Votes

"One of the most significant rule changes in the history of the House" is how the Democratic Study Group termed the House's decision in 1970 to permit twenty members* to request a record vote on any amendment offered in the Committee of the Whole.[17] Prior to this rule revision the House disposed of floor amendments in one of three ways: voice vote, standing vote, or nonrecorded teller vote. An amendment's fate was often decided only after all three procedures had been employed. But in none of these actions did the individual member's position become a matter of public record. When a teller vote was ordered, the chairman of the Committee of the Whole designated two members—the person who had introduced the amendment and its principal adversary (usually the standing-committee chairman)—to "count heads" as the yeas and the nays, in turn, proceeded from the well of the House chamber up the center aisle. When all had been tallied, the tellers announced the result from their position in the rear of the House floor. The fact that a constituent did not know how his or her representative voted under this system often deterred those who favored the amendment from joining the teller line. With nothing to gain at home, they preferred not to alienate those who were in a position to dispense favors—the House leadership and the standing-committee chairman. A high-ranking House member admitted to University of Michigan Professor John W. Kingdon that "we often got commitments from Southern Democrats and even Republicans to just stay away and not vote. Then we'll get the amendment blocked on a teller vote and nobody gets hurt." This approach, Kingdon stated, "was often used to block amendments from the liberal side."[18] This reinforced the DSG analysis, which revealed that under pre-1970 rules the only amendments that passed during floor consideration were those presented by conservatives with "establishment" blessings.[†][19]

My own experience coincides with these findings. Early in 1970 four like-minded members of the Armed Services Committee, representatives Otis G. Pike (D.-N.Y.), Lucien N. Nedzi (D.-Mich.), Robert

---

*Changed to twenty-five Members in 1979.
†In those rare instances before 1971 when the Committee of the Whole, by voice, standing, or nonrecorded teller vote, accepted an amendment that was opposed by

L. Leggett (D.-Cal.), and Robert T. Stafford (R.-Vt.), joined me on several occasions in my office to dissect the Military Procurement Authorization Bill, HR 17123, which was then before our committee. The press eventually dubbed this coalition "The Fearless Five" (although at times many viewed us as the "Foolish Five"). We reached a consensus on eight amendments which, collectively, we would support during the mark-up of HR 17123. Since these amendments had no chance of passage in committee, we prepared ourselves to take them to the House floor, where we figured to find a more sympathetic audience.

To wage any kind of a floor fight, however, we needed staff and organizational assistance. The vehicle that we felt would satisfy this requirement was a confederation to which I belonged, Members of Congress for Peace through Law (MCPL). This bipartisan, bicameral organization had one of the largest congressional memberships (105 in 1970) of any group on the Hill. Since most MCPL members were disposed to our views, they were apprised in advance of the floor consideration of the eight amendments. A "whip" system was created whereby MCPL staff would notify members' offices when a particular "Fearless Five" amendment was being debated on the floor. An estimate was made as to the time the teller vote would be held, and the members were urged to be on the floor at that moment to participate in the count. This tactic was easily countered. Observing the influx of strange faces on the floor, the committee leadership simply prolonged the discussion. In time, the "Fearless Five" supporters left the chamber, and when the prospective head toll looked favorable, Committee Chairman L. Mendel Rivers (D.-S.C.) called for a vote.

Under these circumstances, to paraphrase my World War II commander, General Joseph Stilwell, we "took a hell of a licking." Leggett's proposal to delete funds for the Anti-Ballistic Missile (ABM)

---

the standing-committee chairman handling the bill, a recorded roll call, if supported by members, could be ordered after the body resumed sitting as the House. This rule still pertains today. However, since under current procedures a recorded vote on an amendment already has been taken in the Committee of the Whole, there is little reason for the leadership to request a second vote in the House unless the outcome of the initial balloting was extremely close. A little "arm-twisting" during the interim between the two votes is sometimes sufficient to reverse the previous decision.

lost 85–131 (with 219 not voting). Nedzi's efforts to scrap $100 million for research on the B-1 bomber fell 51–91. Our other six amendments were defeated by margins of 48–90, 86–128, 21–58 (standing vote), 132–215, 22–55 (standing vote), and 30–72 (standing vote). Fourteen other amendments met the same fate. However, in a move that seemed to confirm the conclusions of the DSG, Chairman Rivers did accept one amendment, a motion offered by a conservative Republican, Louis C. Wyman of New Hampshire.

At approximately the same time that Mendel Rivers was demonstrating how the unrecorded teller vote worked to a committee chairman's advantage, the Rules Committee was in the final stages of preparing a congressional reorganization package for House consideration. By a 6–6 vote the panel rejected efforts to incorporate in its bill a recorded teller vote provision. The reformers, therefore, took their case to the floor.

On July 27, 1970, Congressman Thomas P. "Tip" O'Neill, Jr., a Democrat from Massachusetts who was ultimately to ascend to the speakership, offered the recorded teller vote amendment on behalf of his cosponsor, Representative Charles S. Gubser (R.-Cal.), and 180 other colleagues. "Our duties to the Nation and to the people we represent," declared O'Neill, "make this amendment necessary. We are primarily and most importantly legislators. And if the work of legislation can be done shrouded in secrecy and hidden from the public, then we are eroding the confidence of the public in ourselves and in our institutions. . . . There should be no one among us who is not willing to go on record on the vital issues of the day, . . . who is unwilling to go to his constituents on this record—his true record, based on the important votes in the Committee of the Whole."[20]

The House, ironically, accepted this amendment by a voice vote. When the new procedure became operative in 1971, members were given twelve minutes (later changed to fifteen minutes) to answer the two bells signifying a recorded teller vote. Provision was also made for recording all votes and quorum calls by "electronic device" (voting machines placed on the House floor), a practice that was implemented in 1973.

Strengthened House Capacity to Deal with the Executive Branch

Technological Independence

On May 11, 1971, I appeared on CBS's "Sixty Minutes" show as a foil for Mike Wallace. Wallace was investigating the operational failure of the Mark-48 torpedo which Congress had authorized the navy to procure several years previously. Wallace inquired how we on the Armed Services Committee (to which I was assigned at the time) knew whether the Mark-48 would work. "Lacking the expertise," I replied, "we don't have the competence . . . or the time to investigate. . . . So, unfortunately, it is on faith in many instances." To which Wallace responded, "You seem to be saying that the men who have to vote billions of dollars for these weapons, simply don't have the facts to vote intelligently." "That's correct," I answered.[21]

Wallace's criticism was not lost upon the Congress. To strengthen its research capabilities the House, during the 1970s, authorized substantial staff increases. By the end of 1979, the Foreign Affairs Committee staff had grown from twenty-four to seventy-nine. Members' personal staffs expanded from a maximum of thirteen in 1969 to eighteen permanent and four supplemental in 1980. Whereas in 1969 I had had no legislative assistants, at the time I left Congress in 1978 I had six on my district payroll and one on the Foreign Affairs Committee.

Congress also moved to extend its technological reach. After five years of study the Committee on Science and Astronautics brought to the House floor on February 8, 1972, HR 10234, which established an Office of Technology Assessment for the Congress. Representative Charles A. Mosher (R.-Ohio) argued the case for congressional technological independence:

> Let us face it, Mr. Chairman, we in the Congress are constantly outnumbered and outgunned by the expertise of the executive agencies. We desperately need a stronger source of professional advice and information, more immediately and entirely responsible to us and responsive to the demands of our own committees in order to more nearly match those

resources in the executive agencies. . . . We need to be much more sure of ourselves, from our own sources, to properly challenge the agency people, to probe deeply their advice, to more effectively force them to justify their testimony—to ask the sharper questions, demand more precise answers, to pose better alternatives.[22]

"The OTA," Representative John W. Davis (D.-Ga.) stated during the debate, "would not itself carry out technological assessments, but would arrange for them to be done through contract with appropriate outside groups—industrial, nonprofit, academic, or ad hoc. Such assessments would be undertaken upon request of any congressional committee or upon the initiative of the Director of the office or its [thirteen-member] governing board. The office should be valuable not only in updating the machinery of Congress for dealing with technological issues, but in improving the congressional image with regard to legislative efficiency."[23]

Despite some fears that Congress was creating "another bureaucracy," the House approved HR 10243 by a 256–118 margin. After Senate passage HR 10243 was signed into law by President Nixon on October 13, 1972.

The next step in enhancing its technical capabilities came when the House proceeded to make scientific innovation available to its individual members and their staffs. As Stephen E. Frantzich pointed out, "On the aggregate level the House of Representatives in recent years adopted system wide computer applications for its payroll, the tracking of legislation, bibliographic and original research through the Library of Congress and the Congressional Reference Service, committee and floor scheduling, economic and tax simulations, access to executive branch and commercial data files, and the electronic voting system."[24]

Frantzich suggested, however, that "the real innovative step for the individual member is to install his own terminal. The House as an institution," noted Frantzich, "has encouraged computer applications by individual members through funding, pilot projects, selective benefits, information exchange and training."[25] In 1975 House rules were changed to enable members to use up to one thousand dollars per month from their office allowances for computer-related services. Three years later this spending limitation was removed when the House decided to permit unrestricted use of individual office accounts. "As we move into a world with an exponential rate of change, Congress," Frantzich concluded, "is not necessarily doomed to the laggard position."[26]

War Powers

Congress has used its war powers sparingly. Only five times has the legislative branch resorted to a declaration of war: the War of 1812, the Mexican War (1846–48), the Spanish-American War (1898), World War I (1917–18), and World War II (1941–45).

By contrast, the president, according to a Library of Congress study, by 1975 had employed our armed forces in skirmishes abroad in 183 instances without any formal authorization from Congress.[27] In some cases the chief executive simply declined to await congressional sanction, because of his fear that the legislative branch, by its very nature, was unable to respond promptly or coherently to emergencies. On other occasions, as the Library of Congress's Louis Fisher observed, the president "has invoked that vague prerogative" of protecting American life and property abroad "to satisfy much larger objectives of the executive branch."[28] This has been especially true during the post–World War II period, a time in which the United States has been forced to assume infinitely greater international responsibilities.

In legal suits contesting these military interventions, the president, in his capacity as commander in chief, has been given wide latitude by the courts. Fisher suggested that the Supreme Court "has been unwilling to intrude its judgment as to when war begins and ends."[29] Asked to rule on the legality of the Vietnam War, the Supreme Court consistently handled the issue as a "political question to be resolved by Congress and the President."[30] A federal district court held that, by appropriating funds to maintain our presence in Vietnam, Congress ipso facto legitimized our military mission there.

Many of us in Congress felt that somehow a bridge had to be erected over this constitutional war-powers chasm. Spurred by growing national disapproval of the Indochinese conflict, the House of Representatives in 1970, 1971, and 1972 approved three separate resolutions that sought to define, by statute, the issues left unanswered by Article 1, Section 8, and Article 2, Section 2, of the Constitution. After Senate-House conferees failed to take action on these measures, the House, in 1973, passed another, much stronger, proposal which, when reconciled with a similar Senate version, became the War Powers Resolution of 1973.

The War Powers Act, which, as mentioned previously, was passed over President Nixon's veto, has several important provisions:

> It allows the president to introduce armed forces into hostile situations only when granted specific congressional authority or, in the absence of legislative approval, when the United States, its territories, its possessions, or its armed forces come under enemy attack.

> It orders the president to consult "in every possible instance" with Congress before undertaking such a commitment.

> It directs the president, when exposing American service personnel to actual or potential enemy fire without specific legislative authority, to report in writing to Congress within forty-eight hours after taking such a step.

> It requires that the president "within sixty calendar days after a report is submitted or required to be submitted . . . shall terminate any use of United States Armed Forces with respect to which such report was submitted unless the Congress has declared war or has enacted a specific authorization for such use of United States Armed Forces."

> It permits the president to extend the original sixty-day period for not more than an additional thirty days if he "determines and certifies to the Congress in writing that unavoidable military necessity respecting the safety of United States Armed Forces requires the continued use of such armed forces in the course of bringing about a prompt removal of such forces."

> It empowers the Congress "at any time that United States Armed Forces are engaged in hostilities outside the territory of the United States, its possessions and territories without a declaration of war or specific statutory authorization" to direct the president, by a concurrent resolution (which is not subject to his veto), to remove such troops.[31]

Cecil V. Crabb, Jr., and Pat M. Holt, in their publication *Invitation to Struggle*, lauded the War Powers Resolution as a measure which, "as much as any other step taken by Congress in recent years,

. . . symbolized legislative disenchantment with the 'imperial presidency' and a determination to become an equal partner with the executive in the foreign policy process."[32]

Congressional Fiscal Policy

During each of my fourteen years as an economics instructor I devoted several class hours to a discussion of federal fiscal policy. I would relate to my students how Congress utilized the budget as a countercyclical tool, deliberately prescribing a deficit to combat recession and unemployment or generating a surplus to abate demand-inspired inflation.

When I arrived in Congress, however, I discovered that any resemblance between the fiscal theory that I had taught and that actually practiced by the legislative branch was "purely coincidental." There was no congressional "budget." Instead, Congress considered fifteen separate appropriations bills, plus one or more annual supplemental appropriations, which were unrelated to any total expenditure level and were in no way coordinated with anticipated federal revenues. This meant that Congress could not know what the government would spend in any given fiscal year until the last appropriations bill had cleared its calendar (which usually occurred six months into the new year). This, of course, made it impossible for Congress to use the budget to influence the direction of the economy or to set national priorities.

In his annual budget message to the Congress, released on January 29, 1973, President Nixon detailed Congress's deficiencies in its approach to fiscal policy:

> The fragmented nature of congressional action often results in a still more serious problem. Rarely does the Congress concern itself with the budget total or with the effect of its individual action on those totals. Appropriations are enacted in at least 15 separate bills. In addition, "backdoor financing" in other bills provides permanent appropriations authority to contract in advance of appropriations, authority to borrow and spend without an appropriation, and program authorizations that require mandatory spending whether or not it is desirable in the light of current priorities.[33]

Nixon used these concerns as the pretext for refusing to spend monies appropriated by the legislative branch to carry out programs that he personally opposed. At one time the Nixon administration withheld as much as $18 billion in funds voted by Congress for specific purposes.[34]

Senator Charles Mathias (R.-Md.) expressed the resentment of most members of Congress when he testified on March 24, 1974, before the Senate Judiciary Committee's Subcommittee on the Separation of Powers: "We cannot allow the President or the executive branch to have an informal line item veto of appropriated money which cannot be overriden. This is, in effect, to impound declared congressional policy and threaten Congress' very existence."[35]

Determined to thwart Nixon's growing tendency to ignore its budgetary dictates, the House, on July 25, 1973, passed HR 8480 which would have allowed Congress to set aside any presidential impoundment. This bill, however, faced a certain veto, which in all probability, would be sustained. Confronted with this prospect, and recognizing Congress's vulnerability to charges of "fiscal irresponsibility," Representative Richard Bolling (D.-Mo.) moved in the House Rules Committee to attach the provisions of HR 8480 to a budget reform proposal that his committee then was considering. This amalgam became the nucleus of the Congressional Budget Act of 1974, initially approved by the House on October 5, 1973.

As finally cleared by the Congress on June 18, 1974 (when the House adopted the conference report), the Congressional Budget Act:

> Creates the Congressional Budget Office and separate House and Senate budget committees.
>
> Changes the fiscal year from July 1–June 30 to October 1–September 30.
>
> Orders the president to submit a "current services budget" (the cost of ongoing activities if maintained at their present level) to Congress by November 10 of each year and his annual budget message by the fifteenth day after Congress reconvenes.
>
> Sets a March 15 deadline for committees and subcommittees to transmit proposed program summaries to the budget committees.
>
> Calls for congressional completion by May 15 of the First

Concurrent Budget Resolution which, for the forthcoming fiscal year, sets targets for expected receipts, anticipated cash outlays and spending authority by functional categories, and projected results—a budget in surplus, balance, or deficit.

Directs standing committees to report all authorizing legislation by May 15.

Establishes the seventh day after Labor Day as the date on which Congress must complete action on all appropriations bills.

Requires Congress to approve by September 15 the Second Concurrent Budget Resolution, which sets binding income, expenditure, obligational authority, and overall operational (surplus/deficit) goals.

Mandates passage by September 25 of any reconciliation bill that may be necessary to bring previously authorized spending and revenue actions into conformity with the final budget resolution.

Imposes controls on "backdoor spending" by limiting entitlements to that amount allocated in the most recent budget resolution and by subjecting to points of order any new authorization whose funds are not covered in a subsequent appropriation bill.

Authorizes the president to rescind appropriations only when Congress passes a resolution supporting such action (in the absence of a resolution, the money must be spent within forty-five legislative days).

Permits the president, without congressional approval, to defer expending appropriated funds for all or part of a fiscal year.

Allows Congress to terminate such deferrals by passage of an appropriate resolution by either chamber.[36]

In the opinion of *National Journal* reporter Joel Havemann, "the most clearly defined purpose of budget reform was to allow Congress to control presidential impoundments."[37] But, conceded Havemann, "the bulk of the reform established procedures to enable Congress to approach the budget as a statement of economic policy and spending priorities."[38]

Restrictions on Cash Sales of Military Equipment and Services.

The report on the Foreign Assistance Act of 1974 issued on October 25, 1974, by the House Foreign Affairs Committee noted that "foreign military sales are an important tool of U.S. foreign policy and in many cases have a direct impact upon our relations with both the purchasing country and on its neighboring countries as well."[39]

Each year Congress authorizes government-to-government sales of defense articles and services to "friendly foreign countries and allies."[40] Although it did set an overall ceiling on the amount of credit sales, Congress imposed no limitations on cash sales before 1974.

While the Congress was furnished each year with a projection of military cash sales, the House Foreign Affairs Committee found this information "inaccurate and unreliable."[41] In fiscal 1974, for example, the Department of Defense estimated that cash sales would reach $3.6 billion. Instead, they totaled $5.9 billion. This difference, the Foreign Affairs Committee felt, "clearly demonstrates the need for timely reporting by the executive branch."[42]

This led to the adoption during the committee's mark-up of the 1974 Foreign Assistance Authorization Bill of an amendment submitted by Representative Jonathan B. Bingham (D.-N.Y.) that required the president to give advance notice to the Congress of any offer to sell defense articles or services that cost over $25 million. The amendment further provided that the "letter of offer shall not be issued if the Congress, within twenty legislative days after receiving any such statement, adopts a concurrent resolution stating in effect that it objects to such proposed sale." This stricture would not apply if the president certified "that an emergency exists which requires a sale in the national security interests of the United States."*[43]

In adopting the Bingham proposal the committee believed that it would "give Congress more effective control over the amount of defense articles sold each year."[44] While not automatically triggering legislative action, the amendment, the committee maintained,

---

*In 1976 the reporting figure was reduced to $9 million and the period for congressional reaction was increased to thirty days.

would "give Congress the opportunity to study the circumstances surrounding each major sale and to assess the foreign policy impact of each such transaction."[45]

CIA Covert Activities

During hearings that were conducted in March–April 1973 the Senate Foreign Relations Committee's Subcommittee on Multinational Corporations elicited evidence which linked, at least peripherally, the Central Intelligence Agency with efforts to influence the outcome of Chile's 1970 presidential election. This, and other revelations, sparked congressional fears that the CIA was embarking on its own independent foreign-policy initiatives.

In reporting the Foreign Assistance Act of 1974, the House Foreign Affairs Committee acknowledged that "there is a wholly legitimate need for secrecy in carrying out certain activities and operations abroad in order to protect the national security interests."[46] But, insisted the committee, "the Congress, as the elected representatives of the American people, have a right and responsibility to be informed about foreign policy and national security implications."[47]

This premise underlay the committee's acceptance of the late Leo J. Ryan's (D.-Cal.) amendment which, until its repeal in 1980, restricted the CIA's use of monies authorized by the Foreign Assistance Act or any other federal law. Ryan's proposal prohibited the CIA from using funds for operations in foreign countries, "other than activities intended solely for obtaining necessary intelligence, unless the President finds that such [covert] operation is important to the national security of the United States and reports, in a timely fashion, a description of the nature and the scope of such operation" to the appropriate committees of Congress "including the Senate Foreign Relations Committee and the House Foreign Affairs Committee."[48] In this way, suggested the committee, "a foundation for a more effective relationship between the Congress and the Central Intelligence Agency" is established.[49]

Limitation on Reallocation of Foreign Assistance Funds

Congress's annual foreign economic and military assistance budgets reflect only total dollar sums by category. The country-by-country figures upon which these aggregates are predicated appear only in the "back-up" material that the executive branch presents each year to the authorizing and appropriating committees.

Many spending plans, however, become distorted in the time between departmental and agency presentations to congressional committees and the actual disbursement of funds in the field. The administration, therefore, sometimes diverted cash from programs that Congress had earlier informally endorsed.

To limit these "inconsistencies," the House Foreign Affairs Committee in 1974 placed a 10-percent limitation on reallocations for economic development assistance, as well as military aid and security-supporting assistance. This curb could be exceeded only if the president notified the Congress thirty days in advance of the date on which the funds were reobligated. In the case of monies for military aid and other activities involving the recipient nation's security the president "must also determine and report to Congress that the additional assistance is in the security interests of the United States."[50] This provision, commented the committee, "represents part of an overall effort to strengthen Congressional control over the foreign aid program and restrict the President's discretionary power over foreign aid matters."[51]

The flexibility of the executive to transfer funds was further reduced in 1977 when Congress "barred the obligation of any funds in an account to which they were not appropriated without written prior approval of the Senate and House Appropriations Committees."[52]

☆ ☆ ☆

The Institutional and Foreign-Policy Impact of the House Reforms of the 1970s

For the House of Representatives its "decade of reform" ended at 10:03 A.M., December 31, 1979, when Norman Y. Mineta (D.-Cal.) moved that "the House do now adjourn until Thursday, January 3, 1980, at 11:55 A.M."[53]

In a marked departure from Sam Rayburn's exhortation for submissiveness to institutional authority, House members had displayed new aggressiveness during the ten-year period 1970--79 and had substantially altered their place of business and working conditions. These reforms and the vigor with which they were implemented had inspired hope that improved legislative performance would follow. But procedural changes are no guarantee of better operational results. Instead, they sometimes produce unforseen negative consequences. This, unfortunately, was the case when the House, during the 1970s, modified its internal rules: the institution and its capacity to conduct its foreign-policy responsibilities were weakened, and this, in turn, led to actions that ill-served our nation's interests abroad.

CHAPTER 4

The Reforms Take Effect

Of those who chaired House committees in 1969, only two, Harley O. Staggers (D.-W. Va.) and Carl D. Perkins (D.-Ky.), served in the Ninety-sixth Congress (1979–80). When asked how heading a committee in 1980 differed from performing as chairman a decade earlier, Staggers replied: "Changes have slowed down the process. A chairman formerly could set the agenda. Now a bill must go to a subcommittee for a hearing and markup and then to the full committee for final action. The many amendments offered on the floor slow things down even further to a point where it is difficult to get anything done."[1]

The figures corroborate this characterization of the "new" House. Between 1969 and 1979 the chamber's work load greatly increased, while its legislative output declined. In 1979 the House met for a total of 747 hours and 21 minutes, answered 177 roll calls, and enacted 190 public laws.[2] To produce 187 public laws in 1979, House members sat in session for 974 hours and 54 minutes and cast 672 electronically recorded votes.[3] These numbers become even more significant when we consider the effects of the reforms on the three areas outlined in chapter 3 as targets of the House reform effort.

Decentralization of Power within the House

Committee Appointments

During the first two terms of his speakership, "Tip" O'Neill was reluctant to use the leverage that his committee appointive powers offered. For instance, he did not exercise his option to remove "unfriendly" Democrats from the Rules Committee (probably because of the threat of removal, Rules Committee Democrats have generally been supportive of the House leadership). Further, the speaker, during the Ninety-sixth Congress, attempted to preserve the regional balance of the rules-making body by replacing departing New York, California, and Texas Democrats with solons from the same three states. In his only sectional switch, O'Neill named a South Carolinian to fill a seat vacated by a Washington State retiree. Those four appointments, incidentally, did nothing to strengthen the speaker's grip on the Rules Committee. The overall Party Unity* scores of the three selectees who served in the Ninety-fifth Congress were less than those of their predecessors and, in two cases, were below the overall Democratic average for the House of Representatives.

Nor did the Steering and Policy Committee, during the period 1975–80, utilize its prerogatives as the Committee on Committees either as a "carrot" or as a "stick." Its ability to reward and punish, of course, is constrained by the appointment guarantees stipulated in section M1. E of the caucus manual. More important, the principal goal of the Steering and Policy Committee, in the view of several Hill staff members, was to "keep the Members happy." A survey conducted in 1980 by University of Kansas professor Burdett A. Loomis attested to the success of that effort. Third-term members (those first elected in 1974) responding to his questionnaire showed a "Major Committee Assignment Satisfaction Rating" of 100 percent (Highly Satisfied, 55 percent; Somewhat Satisfied, 45 percent).[4]

The makeup of 1979 committee rosters is another proof that a "keep them happy" principle motivated the House leadership. Six freshmen (as opposed to none in 1969) and seven sophomores (contrasted with three in 1969) sat on the House's three "exclusive committees." Six newly elected members were named to the Foreign Affairs Committee in 1979, whereas only one freshman had received that assignment in 1969. Fifty-six other newcomers were placed on major committees at the beginning of the Ninety-sixth Congress: Agriculture, seven; Armed Services, five; Banking, Finance, and Urban Affairs, seven; Education and Labor, eleven; Interstate and Foreign Commerce, seven; Judiciary, six; Public Works and Transportation, thirteen. Obviously, the large number of Con-

---

*The *Congressional Quarterly Almanac* (*CQA*) defines Party Unity votes as those which split the parties, a majority of voting Democrats opposing a majority of voting Republicans. Votes on which either party divides evenly are excluded.

gressional "dropouts"—voluntary and involuntary—in 1976 (sixty-seven) and 1978 (seventy-seven) made it infinitely easier for the appointing authorities of both parties to mollify the House's "underclassmen."

Committee Chairmen

The profile of 1979 House committee leaders, thanks to the retirement of seventeen of the Ninety-first Congress's nineteen chairmen,* was somewhat different from that of their 1969 counterparts. Average age in 1979 was 62.6 years.[5] Regionally, the balance shifted from southern and middle Atlantic states to the East Coast, the Middle West, and the Pacific Coast, each of which claimed five chairmen. Philosophically, the 1979 crop of committee dons was somewhat less conservative than their 1969 predecessors. Their Conservative Coalition Support† in 1979 was 33.7 percent,[6] whereas in 1969 the Conservative Coalition Support of the committee chairmen had been 45.4 percent.[7] And, while losing some of its rigidity, the seniority system still remained an important criterion for reaching the top rung of the committee ladder. Thus, twenty of the twenty-two House chairmen in 1979 had the longest tenures on their committees. The senior members of the Merchant Marine and Fisheries and Small Business committees, Thomas L. Ashley (Ohio) and Tom Steed (Okla.), deferred to John M. Murphy (N.Y.) and Neal Smith (Iowa). In lieu of committee chairmanships, Ashley and Steed preferred to retain more powerful subcommittee chairs on the other standing committees on which they served.

It is authority, the staff of life for the chairman of yesteryear, which underwent the most radical change after 1969. To their dismay, several previously impervious committee leaders learned from a vengeful caucus that "seniority, alone, does not a chairman make." The caucus's own version of the "Saturday Night Massacre" occurred on January 16 and 22, 1975, when it dethroned three reigning commit-

---

*The twentieth chairman, Richard H. Ichord (D.-Mo.), also served in the Ninety-sixth Congress, but the Internal Security Committee, which he headed in 1970, was abolished by the House in 1975.
† *CQA* defines the "Conservative Coalition" as a voting alliance of Republicans and Southern Democrats against the Northern Democrats in Congress.

tee chairmen, F. Edward Hebert (La.-Armed Services), W. R. Poage (Tex.-Agriculture), and Wright Patman (Tex.-Banking, Currency, and Housing). On January 26, 1977, Robert L. F. Sikes (Fla.), who a year earlier had been reprimanded by the House for alleged conflict of interest and failure to meet security disclosure requirements, was deposed by the caucus as chairman of the House Military Construction Appropriations Subcommittee. Incidentally, in 1979 the caucus rejected two Steering and Policy Committee recommendations for the Budget Committee, Sam B. Hall, Jr. (Tex.), and Joseph L. Fisher (Va.), and in their place chose representatives Wyche Fowler (Ga.) and James R. Jones (Okla.).

Because of these caucus "lynchings," House chairmen, a DSG study suggested, "were suddenly responsive and even solicitous not only to members of their own committees but to members generally."[8] This undoubtedly explains Loomis's finding that 78 percent of those legislators who answered his 1980 questionnaire expressed satisfaction with the chairs' sharing of committee responsibilities. This is a 12-percent improvement over the rating of chair cooperativeness by respondents to a survey in 1976.[9]

But threat of decapitation by the caucus is not the only burden that the chairman must bear. Chairmen have "lost the right," observed political science professors Lawrence C. Dodd and Bruce I. Oppenheimer, "to determine the number, size, and majority party membership of subcommittees, . . . to appoint subcommittee chairs, to control referral of legislation to subcommittees, or to prevent their committees from meeting. . . . Finally, as a result of the growth of subcommittee activity, many . . . defer to the subcommittee chairpeople in the management of legislation."[10]

In the realm of foreign policy the accuracy of this commentary can be validated by tracing the history of legislation considered in the Foreign Affairs Committee in 1969 and 1979. In the former year neither of the two major bills upon which the committee acted was referred to a subcommittee. In 1979 nine of eleven key measures were transmitted initially to Foreign Affairs subcommittees.

Committee chairmen, nonetheless, have not been silenced. In fact, in 1979 the number of foreign policy proposals they handled on the floor (sixteen of thirty) actually increased over that handled in 1969 (five of fourteen). This may have been a mixed blessing, however, for in 1979 managers of international relations bills combatted an unprecedented barrage of amendments.

Also, committee heads still retain many of the perquisites that they enjoyed in 1969. Staff appointments is one. In 1969, Representative Thomas L. Morgan (D.-Pa.) cleared all of the twenty-four slots allotted to the Foreign Affairs Committee, which he chaired. Although by 1979 Chairman Clement J. Zablocki (D.-Wis.) had begun sharing the staff-appointing authority with ranking minority member William J. Broomfield (Mich.) and eight subcommittee chairmen, his office in 1979 still controlled forty-nine positions, twenty-five more than Morgan.[11]

Chairman Zablocki (as do the other committee leaders) still determines the time and dates of hearings and directs the committee during its discussions. However, as "Doc" Morgan discovered in 1974 when confronted with the Hamilton-Whalen ad hoc group, committee "followership" has wilted in the face of the House's new openness. For instance, on June 5, 1980, when the House considered the Fiscal Year 1981 Foreign Aid Authorization Bill (HR 6942), a substantial number of committee members deserted Zablocki during votes on three floor amendments that he strongly opposed but which ultimately carried. The most harmful in Zablocki's eyes, a $786-million authorization reduction, attracted thirteen foreign-affairs panelists (five Democrats, including one subcommittee chairman, and eight Republicans). Fourteen committee Democrats (including six subcommittee leaders) and ten Republicans supported the motion to eliminate Economic Support Funds for Syria, while five Foreign Affairs Democrats (including two subcommittee heads) and ten Republicans joined the move to reduce aid to Zambia.[12] The $786-million spending cut had not been offered in committee, while the Syrian and Zambian proposals had been defeated 5–8 and 5–11, respectively, by an unrecorded "show of hands" in committee. This indicates just how vincible a chairman can become when his members are forced to "go on record."

Subcommittee Chairmen

"Whenever you scratch a House Democrat," said Congressman Jim Oberstar (D.-Minn.), "you scratch a chairman."[13] Oberstar was at least half correct. Thanks to caucus manual rule M2. B, 54 percent of the House Democrats in 1979 were addressed as "Mr. Chairman." That figure includes 139 individual subcommittee chairs plus the nine standing and select committee leaders who headed no subcommittee (but does not count the Budget Committee's 1979 task force chairmen). In the Ninety-sixth Congress only six Democrats occupied two subcommittee chairs. Another, Representative Charles Rose (N.C.), directed three subcommittees. However, these breaches of the "one-per-member" limitation were only apparent, for the House Administration Committee and the Select Committee on Intelligence were exempt from the rule.

Caucus rules changes produced two other important effects on the selection of subcommittee chairmen. First, length of time on a subcommittee as a prerequisite for a chairmanship has been reduced. Second, many subcommittee chairmen have been elevated to their posts from the lower tiers of the committee tables. The meteoric rise of Julian C. Dixon (D.-Cal.) to a subcommittee chairmanship exemplifies this new mobility. In 1980, in the middle of his first term, he was named chairman of the Appropriations Committee's District of Columbia Subcommittee, succeeding Charles Wilson (D.-Tex.), who gave up his seat to move to the more prestigious Defense Subcommittee. Dixon was thirty-fifth in the line of thirty-six committee Democrats. Two of the eight subcommittees of the Foreign Affairs Committee were led by third-termers Stephen J. Solarz (N.Y.) and Don Bonker (Wash.), who ranked eleventh and twelfth among committee Democrats.

While committee seniority remains the starting point in the race for subcommittee leadership, the bidding procedure prescribed by rule M5. A of the caucus manual makes the contest more competitive. In 1979 three junior Democrats successfully challenged more senior members for subcommittee chairs. Henry A. Waxman (Cal.), tenth ranked on the Interstate and Foreign Commerce Committee, defeated seventh-ranked Richardson Preyer (N.C.) for the chairmanship of that committee's Health Subcommittee.* In another Interstate and Foreign Commerce Committee battle sixth-ranked Bob Eckhardt (Tex.) downed fourth-ranked John M. Murphy. After the first three bidders for the chairmanship of the Environment, Energy, and Natural Resources Subcommittee had been rejected by their

---

*Some charged Waxman with attempting to "buy" his chairmanship by making political contributions to committee Democrats from a campaign fund which he established.

Government Operations Committee colleagues, sixteenth-ranked Toby Moffett (Conn.) eventually was selected.

Finally, with the enhanced jurisdictional status of subcommittees came a growth in the "clout" of their chairmen. Not unusual, therefore, was the story of one subcommittee chairman: "The Administration and the interest groups now pay more attention to me and Congressman _____ [another subcommittee chairman] than they do our committee chairman. They completely by-pass him."

Subcommittee Rights

University of Massachusetts Professor George Goodwin, Jr., has described the subcommittee as a "major locus of decision-making."[14] The Foreign Affairs Committee's eight subcommittees accurately fit this portrayal. Nine of the thirteen proposals over which the committee had sole jurisdiction in 1979 were transmitted to its subcommittees either for mark-up (seven) or policy recommendations (two). A tenth measure was assigned to subcommittee for hearings only (see Table 1).[15] This added legislative responsibility accounted, in part, for the more than doubling of Foreign Affairs subcommittee sessions between 1969 (120) and 1979 (294).[16]

In the past, when hearings were confined to the full committee, those with little seniority often had to wait three to four hours before being recognized to question a witness. As Foreign Affairs subcommittees, each with only six to nine seats, assumed greater legislative jurisdiction, junior members have a much greater opportunity for inquiry, comment, and policy contribution.

New caucus rules have changed the subcommittee's identity in other ways. In 1979 "round-robin" bidding in order of rank equalized the distribution of subcommittee positions to two for each member of the Foreign Affairs Committee.* Twenty-two staff slots were controlled by the eight subcommittee chairmen, and an additional eight staff members were assigned by the minority party to work with Republican subcommittee members. Lastly, in no in-

---

*Chairman Zablocki and ranking minority member Broomfield served on only one subcommittee. Each, however, was an ex-officio member of the other seven subcommittees.

stance in 1979–80 did a Foreign Affairs subcommittee receive a bill from the full committee beyond the two-week deadline established in caucus manual rule M3. A(3).

Greater Openness in House Procedures

Committee and Subcommittee Proceedings

The *CQA* is a lodestone for those investigating congressional procedures. One of its annual features used to be the Special Report on Committee Secrecy. After its 1975 review revealed that only 115 (3 percent) of 3,996 House committee and subcommittee meetings were closed, *CQA* discontinued this special report.[17] My own survey of committee activities in 1979 (subcommittees were excluded from this study) showed that openness was indeed the rule in committee practices. Just 23 of 999 full committee hearings (or 2.3 percent) conducted during the first year of the Ninety-sixth Congress were held in executive session. The Armed Services Committee accounted for 19 of these, while the Ways and Means and Merchant Marine and Fisheries committees each held two closed meetings.

While all of this "sunshine," including televised proceedings, affords expanded publicity opportunities for committee members, its rays could also burn, especially when a representative faces a tough vote that might alienate "the folks back home." Moreover, constituents and representatives of interested groups now have easy access to committee documents. "All one has to do," said a Foreign Affairs Committee staff consultant, "is to go to the front office and tell Molly 'I would like to see the record of H.R._____.'" These transcripts, reminded the consultant, are available even to Soviet Embassy personnel, who, he believed, have not been averse to asking for them.

The 1970s saw a notable rise in the number of full committee meetings. During the last decade Foreign Affairs Committee deliberations increased 130 percent—from 59 in 1969 to 135 in 1979.[18] In many cases those hearings formed a second stage in the legislative process, a time for the full committee to ratify or modify the work of subcommittees. Incidentally, the rule that permitted joint or sequential referral by the speaker enabled the Foreign Affairs

Committee in 1979 to share jurisdiction in the consideration of five other proposals.

Floor Procedures

While the rule permitting committee and subcommittee hearings and floor deliberations to be conducted simultaneously was designed to promote greater House efficiency, it also has proved distracting to members and created an appalling waste of time for administration officials and others called before the committees. When summoned from a committee session to the House chamber for a vote, a representative has to make his decision without benefit of the facts developed during floor debate. Furthermore, five trips in an afternoon from the committee room to the floor (which is not at all unusual) disrupts the continuity of the hearing and leaves witnesses, governmental and private, staring at an empty table for twenty minutes every time the voting bells ring.

During the Ninety-first Congress (1969–70) the same five conferees, three Democrats and two Republicans, were named to three of the four conferences in which the Foreign Affairs Committee was involved. In the fourth conference this quintet was augmented by two senior committee members, one from each party.[19] In 1979, however, thirty-three of the panel's thirty-four members took part in one or more of the nine conferences in which the Foreign Affairs Committee participated.[20] In another departure from earlier practices, the office of the official reporters of committees advised that all nine of these conferences, as well as those in which other standing committees were engaged, were open to the public.[21]

Recorded Floor Amendment Votes

The first major test of the recorded teller vote (now done by an electronic roll-call device) came on March 18, 1971, when the House concurred in an amendment to eliminate funds for further research and development of the supersonic transport aircraft (SST). In a floor speech delivered five days later I remarked that "political scientists may some day term Thursday's proceedings one of the most memorable in Congressional history. Indeed, thanks to last year's rule changes [it] will be remembered as the day when the House of Representatives was returned to the people of the United States."[22] A bit hyperbolic perhaps (something not uncommon among politicians), but somewhat prophetic nevertheless.

The qualitative effects of recording floor amendment votes, especially as they relate to foreign affairs, will be scrutinized in the next chapter. But the quantitative results are easily calculated. Total recorded votes jumped from 177 in 1969 to 672 in 1979. Recorded votes on amendments offered in the Committee of the Whole moved from zero in 1969 to 295 in 1979.* After the Committee of the Whole rose, twenty-three recommittal motions "with instructions" were offered in 1969, of which three were approved. In 1979 all twelve recommittal motions "with instructions" lost.

The ease with which recorded votes on amendments can be secured has contributed to greater member participation in foreign-policy floor debate. In 1969 fourteen foreign-policy bills attracted 44 amendments (see Table 2), of which only 18 were accepted (on a nonrecorded procedure, of course).* In 1979 House members sought to attach 155 amendments to thirty foreign-policy measures, and 104 were approved (see Table 3). This decline in the committee of jurisdiction's floor "batting average" from .591 in 1969[†] to .329 in 1979, while substantial, may be somewhat deceiving, however. A number of amendments in 1979 were directed toward other amendments or in some instances were accepted without quarrel by the bills' sponsors (as was true, also, in 1969). These facts notwithstanding, the floor role of a bill manager has become increasingly frustrating and often embarrassing.

The involvement and effectiveness of noncommittee members in the foreign policy dialogue have also increased. In 1969 sixteen noncommittee representatives introduced 19 amendments to fourteen foreign-policy proposals. Only 6 were adopted. In 1979 thirty-

---

*In 1969, after the membership had reconstituted itself as the full House and the speaker reclaimed his gavel, floor managers asked for separate roll calls on thirteen amendments which were adopted (without a record vote) in the Committee of the Whole. Eleven amendments were reapproved, while two were rejected (thus reversing the action taken in the Committee of the Whole).

[†]In 1970 the committee of jurisdiction's floor performance was even better than in 1969. During consideration of twenty-five foreign-policy bills House members offered a total of eighteen amendments, only three of which passed.

six noncommittee members presented 75 amendments, 45 of which passed (see Tables 2 and 3).

Finally, the proliferation of floor amendments has helped generate more constituent mail and has produced greater lobbying activity. The House postmaster reported that between April 1, 1969, and March 31, 1970, 18,634,520 pieces of mail were delivered to representatives' offices, while in 1979, 45,354,193 pieces were dropped at members' doors.[23] In 1969, 519 lobbying groups, of which 31 were foreign-policy oriented, registered with the clerk of the House. The number filing in 1979 had risen to 760, including 116 with an interest in foreign policy.

Strengthened House Capacity to Deal with the Executive Branch

Technological Independence

The initial impetus for the enlargement of the House staff was defensive—the desire by members to reduce the intellectual advantage enjoyed by the executive branch, which, on any given issue, could send hordes of briefcase-carrying officials to "back up" administration spokesmen testifying on the Hill. But the enhanced analytical capacity produced by this augmenting of personnel soon gave way to a spate of staff-inspired legislative initiatives.

Since many factors contributed to the dramatic increase in the number of proposals considered by the House during the 1970s, it is difficult to establish a precise correlation between that increase and the staff explosion. Nevertheless, as one of my legislative assistants recently confessed to me, "If we were to be worth our salt, we had to come up with something." Generated by my six new legislative assistants and a Foreign Affairs Committee counsel, this "something" consisted of a program of wide-ranging initiatives which I would have been unable to develop or pursue under the staff limitations of 1969.

Although House staff have come under a great deal of criticism in recent publications, it must be remembered that they do not exercise a Svengali-like influence over their "bosses." Rarely, if ever, is a representative moved to sponsor a proposition with which he disagrees. What staff expansion has done, however, is broaden a congressman's participation both in his field of specialization (in my case, the Foreign Affairs Committee) and in those areas where he has little personal knowledge, expertise, or committee involvement.

In 1975 revised House rules enabled me to hire Thomas Popovich, a Brookings Institution economist, as minority counsel of the Foreign Affairs Committee. Popovich's duties included analysis of measures pending before my two subcommittees (International Economic Policy and Africa), preparation of questions to be asked of witnesses, composition of personal statements for inclusion in committee reports, speech writing, and providing a reassuring presence as a "reference source" when I managed committee bills on the House floor. But his most significant role involved legislative strategy, especially the drafting of foreign-policy bills and amendments. Rather than chronicle all of Popovich's undertakings, I will cite two examples of his workmanship, one involving a bill, the other an amendment.

In their book *Foreign Policy by Congress*, Franck and Weisband aptly described the role played by me and Representative Lee Hamilton in creating an "anti-boycott" title to the Export Control Act of 1977 which would be acceptable to pro-Israel lobbies as well as to industrial firms engaged in commerce with Arab nations. Popovich represented me during most of the intricate negotiations with lobbyists, the staffs of their congressional supporters, and the White House. He then helped in the drafting of compromise language which enabled the Foreign Affairs Committee to bring to the floor a bill that incited very little opposition.

During a 1978 study mission to Africa, Popovich and I observed the effects of the rigid interpretation given by our Agency for International Development (AID) field representatives to the "new directions" for economic assistance laid down by Congress in 1973. While emphasizing "people-oriented" projects, this legislation did not forbid the use of foreign-aid funds for infrastructure construction. Too often, however, AID officials took the view that it did, thereby rejecting proposals for low-cost infrastructure construction projects which would have directly benefited the poorest of the poor in countries receiving our aid. Upon our return to Washington, Popovich prepared an amendment to the FY 1979 Foreign Assistance Authorization Bill (HR 12222) which made it clear that

AID could finance certain infrastructure plans within the "new directions" guidelines. The committee unanimously approved this amendment and a complementary one offered by Congressman Solarz.

In 1977–78, thanks to six staff activists, my legislative excursions beyond my committee of jurisdiction far exceeded those of previous years. Some of those endeavors involved sponsorship of bills reflecting legitimate personal concerns of my legislative assistants. For example, one staff member whose husband had recently died became, as she later told me, "obsessed" with the fiscal integrity of our nation's social security system. She formulated a comprehensive bill (along with excellent testimony) designed to improve the fund's solvency by increasing the taxable wage base and restructuring the benefit formula. When it finally marked up the Social Security Financing Bill of 1977 (HR 9346), the House Ways and Means Committee included a provision similar to mine which increased the salary level subject to taxation.

Another legislative assistant, a former rescue squad volunteer, persuaded me to introduce a bill that would permit the families of uncompensated firemen and emergency ambulance attendants who lost their lives in the line of duty to receive the same federal death benefits extended to survivors of paid public servants. Despite the groundwork laid by my staff member, no action was taken on this proposal.

A third legislative assistant, afflicted with an assortment of allergies, interested me in the health problems experienced by many individuals when they ingest certain food ingredients. As a result of articles and committee presentations that he wrote in my behalf, I became Congress's "instant expert" on food labeling and was in great demand as a speaker on that subject, traveling as far as Mexico City to address a group of allergists. Following my departure from Congress, the Food and Drug Administration adopted labeling regulations that embodied many of the provisions that I had earlier advocated.

Among other previously untraveled areas into which the staff moved me in 1977–78 were product liability, congressional payraise deferrals, privacy of medical records, and unregulated telephone monitoring. While all of these initiatives were peculiar to my office, I am sure mine was not a unique experience. Most of the members who served with me in 1977–78 promoted similar staff-incubated bills and amendments, thus contributing to the exponential growth of the House's work load.

In addition to augmenting staff, House members took other measures to ensure themselves better access to information. Individual computer usage was unheard of prior to the changes in 1975 in member allowances. But by 1980, according to Professor Frantzich's study, 75 percent of the House offices operated at least one computer terminal. These offices also availed themselves of the opportunity to enroll in the Member Information Network, which gives direct access to such things as the Member Budget and Library of Congress data bases, the bibliographic citation and major issues files, the Federal Assistance Programs retrieval system, the Justice Retrieval Inquiry System, printouts giving the status of bills currently before the House and summaries of congressional proceedings and debates.[24]

This ability to acquire "instant knowledge" has reduced the member's reliance upon administration experts and committee chairmen. Professor Norman Ornstein described how, during the protracted battle over the 1979 budget, legislators like Dave Obey (D.-Wis.), Marjorie Holt (R.-Md.), and Elizabeth Holtzman (D.-N.Y.) "offered their own economic analyses, often drawing on complex computer simulations of the economy and often contradicting both President Carter and Committee Chairman Robert Giaimo (D.-Conn.)."[25]

War Powers

In his introduction to the report of the Subcommittee on International Security and Scientific Affairs on its 1975 War Powers Compliance hearings, Chairman Zablocki acknowledged that an unspoken consideration of that resolution's sponsors was that "it would require a war to test the statute fully."[26] Fortunately, since this resolution became law in 1973 our country has escaped engagement in any lengthy conflict, thus relieving Congress of the excrutiating task of deciding whether or not to employ the veto option contained in the statute. However, by 1980, three presidents had authorized the use of American personnel, at the cost of forty-nine lives, in nine separate situations to which, arguably, the War Powers Resolution should have applied.

The evacuation of American citizens from Cyprus during the outbreak of hostilities on that island (July 22–23, 1974). Distracted by his impending impeachment, President Nixon was oblivious to the accusations by Senator Thomas F. Eagleton (D.-Mo.) and others that, by not directing a written report to the House and Senate, he had violated the War Powers Resolution.

The Danang (South Vietnam) sealift evacuation (April 3, 1975). A report, dated April 4, 1975, was submitted by President Ford to Speaker Albert in compliance with section 4 of the War Powers Resolution.

The evacuation of Phnom Penh (April 3, 1975). A communication, dated April 12, 1975, was transmitted by President Ford to Speaker Albert pursuant to section 4 of the War Powers Resolution.

The evacuation of Saigon (April 29, 1975). A message, dated April 30, 1975, was conveyed to Speaker Albert by President Ford in compliance with section 4 of the War Powers Resolution.

The attempt to free the crew of the merchant ship Mayaguez, which was captured by Cambodians in the Gulf of Siam (May 14, 1975). In conformance with section 4 of the War Powers Resolution, President Ford transmitted a report to the speaker on May 15, 1975. No mention was made in this message of the deaths of forty-one American servicemen during rescue operations.

The use of CIA personnel in support of two groups involved in the Angolan Civil War (1975–January 1976). President Ford never affirmed that these covert military activities were subject to the reporting clause of the War Powers Resolution.

The evacuation of United States citizens from Lebanon during the course of civil disturbances in that country (June 20, 1976). No report was submitted by President Ford despite the exposure of Department of Defense personnel to proximate danger during the rescue proceedings.

United States airlift of foreign troops and military equipment into Zaire during the Shaba uprising (May 16–June 16, 1978). Despite the vigorous objections of Representative Paul Findley (R.-Ill.), the Foreign Affairs Subcommittee on International Security and Scientific Affairs accepted the Carter administration's contention that, because no "involvement in hostilities was imminent," its Shaba movements did not come within the purview of the War Powers Resolution.[27]

The aborted operation, claiming eight lives, to rescue American hostages being held in Tehran (April 24, 1980). To preserve secrecy the administration did not extend advance notification of the contemplated mission to congressional leaders. On April 25, 1980, President Carter, because of his "desire that Congress be informed on this matter and consistent with the War Powers Resolution of 1973," presented a detailed report of the failed mission to Speaker O'Neill and Senate Majority Leader Robert C. Byrd (D.-W. Va.).[28]

In reviewing the record, one can only conclude, as did *New York Times* correspondent Martin Tolchin, that "Congress has tended to use its new powers more as an ally than a foe of the Administration."[29] Both before and during the military operations, executive consultation was perfunctory, at best, and in one notable case, the Tehran rescue attempt, nonexistent. Very little congressional outcry was heard in those four instances when the requirement that the president report to Congress within forty-eight hours was breached. Even Senator Jacob K. Javits (R.-N.Y.), one of the principal Senate proponents of the War Powers Resolution, declined to challenge President Carter for his refusal to report to Congress during the Shaba action. "On pragmatic grounds," declared Javits, "I let it go. The presence of other troops [brought into Shaba by American military aircraft] was so desirable that for us to say that it was an action in which the U.S. was involved seemed impolitic and impractical."[30]

There appears to be a direct correlation between public opinion polls and Congress's willingness to question presidential military expeditions. After the Mayaguez incident, President Ford's job approval rating soared 12 percent, "one of the sharpest gains ever recorded in Gallup surveys going back to the middle 1930s."[31] In interviews conducted on April 25–26, 1980, Gallup also found that 71 percent felt that President Carter was right in attempting to rescue our hostages in Iran.[32] It undoubtedly was the fear of contradicting public opinion that muted most House members after the

Mayaguez and Tehran casualties were announced. I certainly felt such restraint in 1975 during the Mayaguez affair.

This silent assent, reasoned Tolchin, "raises the specter of future Vietnams in which it took Congress 10 years* to exercise the power of the purse, which it had all along."[33] If such should be our nation's fate, the War Powers Resolution at least ensures that Congress will share responsibility with the chief executive. By creating a process of codetermination, this law divests the legislative branch of any opportunity to disclaim accountability for military action initiated by the president.

Congressional Fiscal Policy

Although some feared that the Congressional Budget Act of 1974 would experience the same early demise that the legislative fiscal reforms of 1946 suffered, this has so far not happened. During its first six years the Budget Act, in fact, served two worthy purposes. First, it helped restore comity between the legislative and executive families by providing a workable mechanism for congressional disposition of presidential decisions to impound appropriated funds. (In 1979 Congress acceded to approximately 80 percent of President Carter's requests for recisions.) Second, the 1974 law forced the House and Senate to make choices—choices involving total spending and income levels and choices regarding categorical priorities.

This latter function, however, is contributing to the steady erosion of the disciplines imposed by the Budget Act. Congress's penchant for avoiding conflict, unfortunately, has left its scars on the new budgetary process. In 1980 Congress missed its Second Budget Resolution target (September 15) by sixty-six days and the First Budget Resolution deadline (May 15) by twenty-eight days. When the Ninety-sixth Congress adjourned on December 15, 1980, it had not completed action on five appropriation bills, including that for foreign assistance. The Second Budget Resolution in 1979 (for fiscal year 1980) did not receive congressional approval until November 28, two months and thirteen days beyond the statutory limit. Although this proposal's overall spending ceiling was exceeded by

---

*Actually, congressional funding of military operations in Vietnam began in 1950.

the sum total of individual appropriations, the House, nonetheless, refused to order its committees to make the cuts necessary to keep within the prescribed aggregate. The House ultimately prevailed in its refusal to invoke reconciliation, but only after Edmund Muskie (D.-Me.), chairman of the Senate Budget Committee, promised that profligate committees would not be rescued by a third resolution.

Delay in passing the second resolution in 1979 stemmed from Congress's dilatory handling of appropriations bills. Seven such measures were not cleared until well beyond October 1, the beginning of the new fiscal year. Three other appropriations bills for fiscal year 1980 were not enacted at all. The Labor-HEW appropriation became ensnarled in the abortion-funding debate. The issue of congressional pay sidetracked the legislative branch appropriation. Only through the passage of continuing resolutions (which permitted expenditures in an amount not to exceed the previous year's levels) did Congress and the Labor and HEW departments continue to operate.

The third money bill to encounter prolonged difficulties that year, the Foreign Assistance Appropriations (HR 4473), bumped into the expenditure ceiling. To remain within the second resolution's cap, Congress finally gave up on HR 4473 and instead approved an emergency funding resolution that continued aid programs either at their 1979 levels or at the House-approved levels for fiscal year 1980, whichever were lower.

Restrictions on Cash Sales of Military Equipment and Services

The key phrase in 1980 among Foreign Affairs Committee members, commented one staff consultant, was "give the President greater flexibility." The Foreign Aid Authorization Bill of 1980, HR 6942, which emerged from the committee on April 16, 1980, reflected this growing deference to the president. Among its provisions were several that made it easier for the commander in chief to provide military assistance without congressional restriction or intervention. As passed by the committee, HR 6942 included the following provisions:

It increased from $10 million to $50 million the amount of military supplies and services that the president can send to friendly countries each year to meet unforeseen emergencies.

It authorized the president to provide up to $250 million in military equipment and services to foreign governments even if that aid is prohibited by other laws, if it is deemed important to United States security.

It limited this $250 million to not more than $50 million per country unless that nation is a victim of communist or communist-supported aggression.

It allowed the president to sell up to $200 million worth of military construction services to foreign governments without congressional approval.

It exempted from congressional concurrence United States arms sales to the NATO states, Japan, Australia, and New Zealand.

It increased from $35 million to $75 million the ceiling on contracts for sales of major defense items which can be marketed commercially without congressional sanction.*

This recidivism had commenced even before 1980. Reflecting Congress's general lack of interest in limiting American arms shipments abroad, United States worldwide foreign military sales grew from $5.9 billion in fiscal year 1974 to $13.0 billion in fiscal year 1979.[34] The exceptions to this malaise occurred when proposed cash sales to certain Middle East states provoked outcries from some interest groups. On these occasions, the House, threatening to use its veto, forced presidential modification of several contracts and the delay or abandonment of others.

One of the earliest executive-legislative confrontations took place when the Department of Defense advised Congress on July 10, 1975, of its intention to ship fourteen batteries of American-made Hawk antiaircraft missiles, valued at $260 million, to Jordan. At the urging of pro-Israeli lobbyists, several representatives filed disapproval resolutions, which the speaker dispatched to the House Foreign Affairs Committee. After the committee adopted Congressman Bingham's

---

* Most of these provisions were retained by the Senate and included in the HR 6942 conference report, which was approved by the House by voice vote on December 2, 1980, and by the Senate, 58–26, the following day. The one significant change was the substitution of the word *vital* for *important* in connection with United States security interests.

resolution of disapproval, President Ford, on July 28, withdrew the sale offer. Subsequently, a new proposal was drafted which stipulated that the missiles could be used only for defensive purposes. This assurance met congressional objections.

Jordan's King Hussein found the new restrictions "insulting," but eventually he grudgingly accepted them. This demeaning treatment by Congress, however, offered Hussein no incentive to accede to our government's requests to mediate, on our behalf, with other Arab leaders to attain peace in the Middle East, a gesture he has repeatedly refused to make. To avoid further congressional embarrassment, he announced in 1981 that Jordan planned to purchase from the Soviet Union, with no strings attached, a $200-million mobile surface-to-air missile system.

Not until October 14, 1981, however, did the House of Representatives actually exercise the veto option authorized by the 1974 Bingham amendment. On October 1, 1981, President Ronald Reagan submitted to the Congress a proposal to sell equipment to Saudi Arabia to enhance that country's air defense capabilities. The $8.5-billion package included five Airborne Warning and Control Systems (AWACS) aircraft, fuel tanks for Saudi F-15 fighters, 1,117 AIM-91 Sidewinder air-to-air missiles, and eight KC-707 aerial refueling aircraft. Anticipating the president's sale announcement, representatives of American Jewish organizations began an intensive lobbying effort in the spring of 1981 to secure a two-house veto of the Saudi deal, arguing that its passage would threaten Israel's national security.

The administration countered by obtaining the endorsement of former presidents Nixon, Ford, and Carter, plus a joint statement by sixteen former high-ranking officials who had served as secretary of state, secretary of defense, national security adviser, or chairman of the Joint Chiefs of Staff under six chief executives. These sixteen national security experts, some of whom had been on opposing sides on other issues, cautioned that "the rejection of this sale would damage the ability of the United States to conduct a credible and effective foreign policy, not only in the Persian Gulf region, but across a broad range of issues."[35] The House failed to heed this bipartisan warning, however, for on October 14 it adopted the resolution of disapproval by an overwhelming 301–111 margin. Repudiating President Reagan were 108 of the 186 Republicans who voted on the resolution. When the battle shifted to the Senate, an unprecedented "one-on-one" personal persuasion effort by the president resulted in several last-minute switches, enabling that body, on October 28, to reject the resolution by four votes, 48–52, thus preserving the sale.

CIA Covert Activities

The House Foreign Affairs Committee's version of HR 6942 also accorded greater "flexibility" to the administration in reporting covert operations by the CIA to the legislative branch. Since its enactment in 1974 the Ryan amendment had been a major irritant to executive branch officials. They argued that briefing members of eight House and Senate committees took an inordinate amount of time and heightened the risk of leaks of sensitive information.

Bowing to this reasoning as well as reacting to growing public sentiment which, in the aftermath of the seizure of our embassy in Iran, called for "unleashing the CIA," the Foreign Affairs Committee reduced from eight to two the number of committees that the president must notify concerning CIA covert actions. On May 28, 1980, during floor consideration of HR 6942, an attempt by Congressman Ted Weiss (D.-N.Y.) to block this change was decisively defeated, 50–325.

Ostensibly, HR 6942 also closed a loophole in the law. The original Ryan provision requiring the president to advise Congress "in a timely fashion" was discarded in favor of language that would permit the chief executive to "defer, for the shortest practicable period, such prior reporting if at the time the report is given the President certifies that such deferral was essential to meet extraordinary circumstances affecting the vital interest of the U.S. or was essential to avoid unreasonable risk to the safety or security of the personnel or methods employed." [36] Despite this new phraseology, there still remained a definitional problem. However, it was left for the president to decide how "the shortest practicable period" differed from "timely fashion." *

---

* The Foreign Affairs Committee's CIA amendment was dropped by the Senate and deleted from the HR 6942 conference report. Instead, similar language was incorporated in S 2597, the Intelligence Agencies Authorization Bill, which received final congressional approval on September 30, 1980.

Limitation on Reallocation of Foreign Assistance Funds

On July 17, 1979, Nicaragua's president, Anastasio Somoza, was top-pled after a protracted guerilla-led civil war. In a move designed not only to meet the needs of this war-torn country but also to gain some degree of influence with its new revolutionary government, President Carter asked Congress on November 9 to include $75 million for Nicaraguan reconstruction assistance in a supplemental appropriations bill. To counter the delays of the appropriation process, Carter also requested that $50 million be reprogrammed from already appropriated funds for immediate use in Nicaragua.

Having already reached its self-imposed aggregate spending ceiling for fiscal 1980, Congress postponed action for eight months on Carter's plea for a supplemental appropriation. Also, relying on the authority that the House Appropriations Committee had arrogated to itself in 1977, two of its members, Clarence Long (D.-Md.) and Charles Wilson (D.-Tex.), effectively foreclosed the written committee approval necessary for the transfer to Nicaragua of previously obligated funds. It was not until July 2, 1980, when Congress enacted HR 7542, the Fiscal Year 1980 Supplemental Appropriations Bill, that Carter's Nicaraguan relief request was granted. But since the authorizing legislation (HR 6081), which cleared Congress on May 19, 1980, prohibited aid if it was found that Nicaragua was assisting terrorist groups, another two months were consumed while the president investigated that possibility. The funds were finally released by the administration on September 18, 1980. These congressionally inspired delays did little to win friends or advance United States interests in Central America, an area which by 1980 was seething with domestic unrest and discontent.

Impact upon Legislative Participants

The House's new modus operandi has created an entirely different environment for those who deal with foreign-policy legislation—particularly for those in the executive branch, the House leadership, and the members themselves. A closer look at each will show how their jobs and life-styles have been altered by a decade of procedural reform.

The Executive Branch

If the number of floor amendments with which it must be concerned is the criterion for judging the executive branch's foreign-policy work load, then its burden increased almost fourfold in the decade considered here (44 amendments in 1969; 155 in 1979). This, of course, is an oversimplification, for the individual legislative packages that the administration's foreign-affairs establishment annually oversees remained relatively static. Yet the executive branch's communication task expanded enormously. White House spokesmen could no longer look to the House leadership or to one or two key committee members to head off potentially embarrassing foreign-policy amendments. Instead, the jurisdictional acquisitions of subcommittee chairmen, the greater opportunities for participation that subcommittees afforded mid-level and lower-ranked members, the newly gained ability (in 1971) to obtain a record vote on floor amendments (and the additional amendments that this generated), the increased involvement in House debate by noncommittee members, and the inclusion of even the most junior members in conferences added to the number of individuals whom the State Department and other agencies had to contact.

Reacting to this growing constituency, the State Department, by 1980, had bolstered its Office of Congressional Relations by adding a third deputy assistant secretary and increasing the number of legislative management officers (LMOs) from six to eleven. "We have also changed our approach to Congress," Deputy Assistant Secretary of State Robert Flaten reported. "Five years ago our LMOs went up to the hill to 'sell.' Today they consider the legislators as partners and, therefore, communicate in both directions, bringing Executive views to Congress and returning to the State Department with Congressional insights."[37]

In Flaten's opinion open committee hearings are a plus for the executive branch. By being permitted to speak (if recognized by the chairman for that purpose) during committee mark-up and conference sessions, administration representatives are often able to head off substantive errors that would have been incorporated in a foreign-policy measure in the days of the closed session. For this reason the State Department began to shift its policy emphasis from committee hearings (when testimony is given before bill-drafting starts) to the later mark-up and conference meetings.[38]

But it is the floor, where radical surgery is performed, that has become the major problem for the executive branch. Even with its expanded liaison team, the State Department lacks the time and resources to reach most representatives. This became abundantly clear during my interviews with forty-six House members.* When asked, "To what extent were you contacted in advance by the executive branch regarding potential 'crippling amendments'?" 37 percent replied "none"; 42 percent, "very little"; 16 percent, "somewhat"; and 5 percent, "considerable."

A New England Democrat complained that the State Department "fails to anticipate these amendments." Two of his Democratic colleagues from Pennsylvania and Michigan not only suffered from pre-vote neglect but received not so much as a "thank you" for their unsolicited support of White House positions.

"They [the executive branch]," contended one GOP member in a 1980 interview, "work only with Democrats." "Even though I don't hear from them," said another minority-party congressman, "I have no loyalty to the Democratic administration anyway." A third Republican, although he never heard directly from executive branch officials, attended a number of State Department briefings, one of which "was helpful in determining my vote on assistance to Nicaragua."

The consequence of this inattention—the acceptance of 104 of 155 floor amendments in 1979—has already been related. In addition to the damage done to pending foreign-policy measures, these legislative setbacks had a chilling effect upon the executive branch's foreign-policy planning. Douglas J. Bennet, Jr., former assistant secretary of state for congressional affairs (later administrator of the Agency for International Development) admitted "that Congressional participation makes a decision to commit U.S. troops abroad less likely. It inhibits extra-legal and covert activities. It makes bold departures less feasible."[39] Of the Shaba airlift, Bennet agreed that "in the old days the planes would have landed in the heart of the

---

* In 1980 I interviewed forty-six members, each of whom was asked the same eight questions. They were selected to conform to the House's overall party, regional, term-in-office, racial, and sex ratios. To avoid any undue foreign-policy bias, I included only two members of the Foreign Affairs Committee. In addition, other House members, as well as committee staff, executive branch officials, and media representatives, were interviewed for the purpose of garnering specific information. All unattributed quotations are drawn from these interviews.

action. The War Powers Act has conditioned the Executive Branch's decision-making process in military crises such as Zaire."[40]

While the results in that situation were salutary, it has been my experience that congressional assertiveness has overly dampened the administration's enthusiasm for developing creative approaches to pressing world problems. Our economic relations with the Third World are an example. As members of the United Nations General Assembly's Third Committee, which deals with global economic issues, United States Ambassador Melissa Wells and I were at a loss to explain to our foreign counterparts our country's international development policies. At the behest of Andrew Young, our permanent representative to the United Nations, Deputy Secretary of State Warren Christopher on November 7, 1977, convened representatives of the State, Treasury, and Commerce departments to review this problem with Young, Ambassador Wells, and me. During our conference these officials repeatedly rejected our suggestions with the response, "Congress won't buy it." This mental paralysis reminded me of what the State Department must have been like during the McCarthy era.

Our government has made no further progress since 1977 in promulgating a comprehensive program to assist developing nations. During a spring 1980 roundtable discussion of the Brandt Commission Report (held at the University of Sussex, Brighton, England), former ambassador Young warned that leadership in North-South issues is not going to come from the United States. "It is important to face the fact," Young said, "that the U.S. is incapable of making a decision at this point. U.S. officials won't even face these questions."[41]

The House Leadership

As we already have seen, the mechanisms crafted to provide a counterbalance to democratization—the Steering and Policy Committee and the speaker's appointive privileges—either have fallen into disuse or have not been utilized effectively. Thus, the leadership's principal task of influencing the content and flow of legislation has become inordinately difficult under revised House rules. This is attributable to three factors.

First, the provisions granting extended powers to subcommittees and their chairmen have created another decision-making layer of 147 separate units. Time and numbers constrain House leaders from overseeing the expanded activities of subcommittees. In their study of majority-party leadership and the effect of decentralization, George Washington University professors Christopher Deering and Steven Smith found that "the majority leadership has yet to establish a systematic relationship with these new power centers. . . . A practice of nonintervention has developed within the leadership regarding subcommittee matters—a practice which is broken only where the leadership program or presidential requests provide an overriding incentive to intervene."[42]

Second, the decision in 1970 to "go public" on amendments offered in the Committee of the Whole has complicated the job of the leadership in several ways. The growth of recorded votes has created more issues with which the leadership must deal. Obviously, time limitations preclude their becoming actively involved in many of these. This assertion was affirmed in my interviews with House members. When queried, "What pressure do you receive from the leadership on pending foreign policy bills and amendments?" 47 percent responded "none," and 53 percent said "very little"; "somewhat" and "considerable" drew zero ratings. And time considerations aside, a member can be asked only so many times to "go to the well" for his or her party leader.

In his book *Majority Party Leadership in Congress*, Professor Randall Ripley pointed to another problem. He concluded that operating conditions for leaders are more effective when members' activities "require less, rather than more, visible action."[43] Although written in 1969, this analysis clearly foretold what lay ahead for the House leadership following the adoption of the O'Neill-Gubser proposal—an abrupt shift in members' allegiances from their leaders to their constituents.

The precursor of this was the previously cited SST vote when a majority of representatives refused to follow the example of the House majority leader, the minority leader, minority whip, and eighteen of twenty-one committee chairmen. Majority Whip "Tip" O'Neill, who on that day broke ranks with his fellow leaders, was himself to experience similar rebuffs after he mounted the speaker's podium in 1977. On two consecutive days in September 1979, he lost five key votes—the Continuing Appropriations Bill, the Second Budget Bill, the Panama Canal Implementation Bill conference report, and a bill increasing the ceiling on the public debt. Afterward, O'Neill was heard to remark, "I think it's gotten out of hand."[44]

A later, less public ignominy was observed by several Democratic members whom I interviewed. On June 12, 1980, O'Neill moved through the well of the House, cajoling fellow Democrats to support the hotly contested FY 1981 First Budget Resolution. He pleaded with John G. Hutchinson, Congress's newest member, who had just won a special election to replace the late John Slack of West Virginia. Concerned about his upcoming race in November, which promised to be close (he had received only 53.8 percent in the June 3 special election), the House rookie turned his back on the speaker, walked to the voting machine, and pulled the "nay" switch.*

While O'Neill was able to collar Hutchinson on the floor, veteran members have learned how to "vote and run." The proximity of several electronic devices to House portals (a distance of approximately five feet) makes it possible for representatives to vote and depart from the chamber within ten to fifteen seconds after entering it. Consequently, while sophisticated computer consoles can pinpoint for the leadership those individuals who have not yet responded to a roll call or who have voted contrary to the party's announced position, any person wishing to avoid "arm-twisting" has an easy avenue of escape.

Third, the dilemmas posed by decentralization and greater member visibility are further complicated by the many nonlegislative functions that leaders are asked to perform. "We have become the prism of attention," suggested former majority whip John Brademas (D.-Ind.). "Political scientists," stated the Indiana legislator, "do not yet realize the amount of time which we must spend meeting with visiting delegations, responding to interviews, delivering addresses to national organizations, attending Washington social and fundraising events, and making campaign speeches in candidates' districts. These great demands on the leadership's time make it more difficult today to lead."[45]

---

*Hutchinson's fears were valid. On November 4, 1980, he was defeated for reelection by ten thousand votes.

The Member

Greater opportunity for self-expression has been the major benefit accruing to individual members from the House reforms of the
1970s. There exists today a more equitable distribution of committee and subcommittee assignments. Leadership positions are more
widely dispersed, thereby drawing more junior representatives into
the circle of legislative authority. Participation in subcommittee,
committee, floor, and conference proceedings has been enhanced.
Floor involvement in foreign-policy discussion, thanks to greater
member staff and information resources, has moved well beyond
the perimeters of the committees of jurisdiction. By providing
the congressman with more eyes, ears, hands, feet, and brain-
power, the staff-information explosion has produced a bill- and
amendment-drafting capability heretofore lacking in the House, enabling him to compete on more nearly equal terms with the executive branch and its representatives.

Offsetting these advantages, members must now work in a more
open atmosphere. Also, they must attend more subcommittee and
committee hearings, spend more days and hours on the House
floor, cast more votes, and, therefore, decide more issues, deal with
more lobbies, and answer more constituent communications. Of
greater concern to individual representatives, however, is that the
House rules changes mean that he or she must take more stands on
issues that could prove damaging with the electorate. The records
of committee votes are now in the public domain. Gone is "the
great advantage of the unrecorded [floor] vote" which enabled the
member to "vote with little or no accountability to his constituents."[46] This, explained veteran Washington radio commentator
Joseph McCaffrey, is why "House members are spending 70 percent
of their time looking over their shoulders."[47]

Perhaps this insecurity, coupled with the insatiable demands of
the job, accounts for the growing incidence of voluntary House re-
tirements (from twelve in 1968 to twenty-seven* in 1976; thirty-
one in 1978; twenty-five† in 1980).

---

*This figure does not include Wayne Hays (D.-Ohio) and James Hastings (R.-N.Y.),
who resigned their seats prior to the end of the Ninety-fourth Congress.
†This figure does not include Daniel Flood (D.-Pa.), Charles Diggs (D.-Mich.), Michael O. Meyers (D.-Pa.), and John W. Jenrette, Jr. (D.-S.C.), who resigned prior to the

Conclusion

In their publication *Congress against Itself,* political scientists Roger Davidson and Walter Oleszek appropriately described the House as "more democratic, more responsive, more accountable, and more open to the public."[48] But at the same time the capacity of House officials to lead has been constricted, the executive branch's ability to "persuade" has diminished, and members have become more vulnerable to the often uninformed judgment of the public they serve.

---

end of the 1980 session, nor does it include Robert Drinan (D.-Mass.), a Jesuit priest who was ordered by the Vatican not to run for reelection.

CHAPTER 5

The House Makes Foreign Policy

Reform is a means to an end, not an end in itself. Unquestionably, for some House members, self-gratification, the "lure of power," was the primary motive for the reforms of the 1970s. But most of us viewed rule and procedural revision as an instrument by which better policy results could be attained and measured our success in those terms.

"The most important policy impact of the reforms," according to the Democratic Study Group, "was on the issue of the Indochina War." The DSG noted that "Caucus instruction of the Democratic members of the Foreign Affairs Committee, adoption of a Caucus policy and position against further funding of the Vietnam war, use of the Steering & Policy Committee, and the record teller reform all played a role in winning House approval in May 1973 of an amendment which cut off funds for the bombing of Cambodia. This was the key congressional action which led to termination of U.S. military involvement in the Indochina war in August of that year." [1]

The recorded teller procedure did make possible that fateful May 10, 1973, vote. But did it contribute to the outcome of that vote? After all, in a key floor vote in 1972 eighty Democrats ignored the caucus edict and opposed the Hamilton-Whalen troop withdrawal amendment. The House, in fact, had fourteen opportunities between January 1971 and May 1973 to use its authorization and appropriations powers to order a halt to our embroilment in Southeast Asia. Instead, in each instance it voted for continued funding of our presence there. By the spring of 1973 all United States ground forces had been withdrawn from Indochina; our only remaining activity there was the bombing of Cambodia by American aircraft.

What the House did on May 10, 1973,* was a relatively unimportant contribution to the winding down of a war which, from our country's standpoint, had about run its course.

So, after twenty-four years of financing the Indochinese conflict, members voted to bow to public opinion, which, by May 1973, strongly disapproved both of our earlier decision to send troops to Vietnam and of our continued bombing of Laos and Cambodia.† This responsiveness to citizen attitudes reflected an "accountability" by House members which they could not have manifested in the prereform era of nonrecorded votes on floor amendments. But this vote, however laudable, also marked a shift in the way the House pursued its foreign-policy objectives.

America's International Commitments

Since 1945, United States foreign-policy goals, and our support for the institutions through which we seek to attain those objectives, have remained constant. Since the days of the Truman Doctrine and the founding of NATO, our national security has been linked with that of Western Europe. A strong Japan is still viewed as a counterweight to potential threats in Asia from unfriendly powers. The United Nations, which we were instrumental in creating, is recognized today, as it was in 1945, as an important organ through which a peaceful resolution of international disputes can be achieved. We continue to support Israel's right to exist, while seeking a just and durable peace in the Middle East. Strategic arms limitations remain a major concern. We maintain our commitment to bilateral foreign assistance, of which the Marshall Plan was a progenitor. As we did in 1944 when they were established at Bretton Woods, we consider the International Bank for Reconstruction and Development (World Bank) and the International Monetary Fund effective ap-

*President Nixon vetoed HR 7447, which contained the Cambodian amendment. Nixon did sign, however, HR 9055, passed by the House on June 29, 1973. This measure ended, as of August 15, 1973, the funding of all United States military operations in Indochina.

†Congress began funding military operations in Vietnam in 1950. According to Dean Acheson our military aid there in 1951 amounted to over half a billion dollars.[2]

proaches to the problems of global poverty and unstable national currencies. The quest begun in the 1930s to reduce international trade barriers continues despite several unfortunate "detours." More recent initiatives have been the resumption of relations with the Peoples Republic of China, the restoration of Panamanian sovereignty over the Canal lands and waterways, and the drive to reduce our dependence upon imported energy.

These goals and directions have been endorsed and pursued by presidents of both parties, and they have had the bipartisan support of the legislative branch. Thus, any disagreements on goals in recent years between Congress and the executive branch have generally not involved substance. Rather, they have arisen over matters of procedure.

Chapter 2 imputes to the Constitution the source of the legislative branch's claim to coequal partnership in the formulation of United States international policies. Throughout this work there have been references to Congress's "reassertion of its constitutional prerogatives" in the area of foreign affairs. It seems appropriate at this point, therefore, to examine just how the House goes about discharging its foreign-policy responsibilities.

☆   ☆   ☆

House Procedures for Handling Foreign-Policy Issues

It is difficult, if not impossible, for Congress to develop a concept and orchestrate it into a cohesive plan of action. The House is a flotilla of 147 subcommittee vessels operating without a compass and led by a skipper who must often bow to the commanders of the individual ships. This situation is further aggravated by overlapping jurisdictions. In 1980 seventeen House standing committees[3] and approximately 56 subcommittees[4] were active in some dimension of foreign policy. This explains why "Congress is not now and never has been well designed to create its own agenda and then act on it in a coordinated way to produce a unified domestic and/or foreign policy program."[5]

This institutional defect has relegated the House to a subordinate role, that of reviewer, rather than initiator, of our nation's approaches to world affairs. It is left to the executive branch to draw the blueprint and erect the framework of our foreign-policy structure. As Table 1 shows, all of the major bills considered by the House Foreign Affairs Committee in 1979 originated with the administration.

In the executive branch only one individual is responsible for foreign policy, whereas in the legislative branch 535 share that responsibility. This means that congressional policy evolves only after a lengthy process involving 535 decision makers and places Congress at a disadvantage in any contest with the chief executive for foreign policy dominance. On any given issue, the executive branch, speaking with one voice, can articulate positions before the fact and move quickly when problems arise. Congress, on the other hand, reacts slowly, often requiring six months to a year to provide a legislative response to a development abroad. During this protracted gestation period representatives can speak only of what they, personally, hope the policy *will be*, not what it is. This cacophony of voices, I discovered, can be very confusing to foreign observers not acquainted with the American constitutional system of checks and balances.

Congress has few vehicles with which, as Congressman Don Bonker expressed it, "to develop any policy or new directions in foreign policy."[6] One of these is the annual Foreign Aid Authorization Bill, which, James Robinson suggested, can be "broadened to include many foreign policy items extraneous to foreign aid, so that the principal committees are usually considering something resembling an omnibus foreign policy program."[7]

The yearly Foreign Assistance Appropriations measure also affords the House an opportunity to write international policy. Because the president lacks the authority to veto specific line items in a money bill, David Truman, former president of the American Political Science Association and Mount Holyoke College, considered an appropriation act a most effective instrument for imposing "a variety of controls on administrative action."[8]

Since the House must depend primarily upon amendments to executive branch proposals to exercise its foreign policy prerogatives, a look at how this system works should be instructive.

The House's Amending Process

After the executive branch takes its stand concerning the manner in which a particular international perturbation should be confronted,* its views, usually accompanied by a draft bill, are conveyed in a written message to the speaker. The speaker then transmits this correspondence to the committee of appropriate jurisdiction. Hearings are conducted, either by the full committee or by a subcommittee, at which time administration representatives are called upon to explain and defend their proposal. Private citizens and members of Congress also may be heard. After all testimony has been presented, the committee or subcommittee, using the draft bill as a benchmark, proceeds with its mark-up in the manner described in chapter 1.

As the Hamilton-Whalen coalition demonstrated, the Foreign Affairs Committee is not uniformly a handmaiden of the State Department. But a committee decision to revise or reject an element of an administration plan is not done precipitously or without forethought. After digesting thousands of words of testimony and often having had an opportunity to meet with leaders of countries that might be affected by a proposed amendment, committee members are usually well aware of the consequences of any policy modification. Also, before an amendment is acted upon, the executive branch is asked to comment and offer suggestions. A compromise frequently results, if the committee or subcommittee accepts the amendment at all.

Although certain committee actions may be vexing to the White House or the State Department, at least the decisions are reached after considerable discussion and negotiation with administration spokesmen. Unfortunately, this is not true for floor amendments. During floor proceedings amendments to a bill are in order after the time allocated by the Rules Committee for general debate has expired (normally one to two hours for foreign-policy measures). After an amendment has been introduced and all discussion has

---

*While the president is held accountable for all executive branch policy, many foreign-policy decisions, of necessity, are made at lower levels. These are often reached only after considerable intra- and inter-departmental infighting. In some cases, of which the absence of a comprehensive Third World development program is an example, no plan of action is forthcoming.

been completed, its sponsor may ask for a recorded vote. If twenty-four colleagues join in this request, a roll call is ordered. Two bells ring, and bedlam ensues.

Since usually no more than thirty to forty members are seated on the House Floor during general debate and consideration of amendments, the other four hundred or so, who now have fifteen minutes in which to record their votes, rush through the five entrances to the House floor like fire horses responding to a four-alarm blaze. On their mad dash from their offices or committee hearings, members have learned from their one-way transistors that they will be voting on "Congressman X's amendment to the Foreign Aid Bill which deletes all funds for country Y." Breathless, the new floor arrival asks his home-state friend, "Why does X want to eliminate assistance for country Y?" "Well," the friend replies, "I wasn't on the floor either, but I did receive a 'Dear Colleague' letter* from X. His arguments seem pretty reasonable, so I think I'll support his amendment."

A real-life example of this "seat-of-the-pants" voting was portrayed by reporter Ed Bruske in the October 21, 1980, *Washington Post*. Bruske's article described the confusion surrounding an amendment offered on August 27 to HR 7998, the Labor, Human Health and Human Services, and Education Appropriations Bill for fiscal 1981.

> Joseph L. Fisher, Northern Virginia's 10th District incumbent Democratic congressman, was finishing a typically light lunch . . . in the House dining room when the familiar ringing bell and flashing light summoned him to a roll-call vote [on an amendment] designed by Rep. John Ashbrook (R.-Ohio) to prevent the Department of Education from using new regulations mandating bilingual education.
>
> Entering the House chamber, the 66-year-old Fisher walked straight to the Democratic floor manager, Rep. William Natcher (D.-Ky.). "I had come steaming in and heard the last little bit of discussion," Fisher recalls. "I went to the desk where the managers of the bill were and I said, 'Let's see a copy of this damn thing. I've never heard of it.'" "Vote against

---

*A member often circulates a mimeographed letter among his colleagues a day or so in advance of the date scheduled for consideration of the bill that he plans to amend. The letter describes the proposed amendment and cites reasons why the author believes it should be adopted.

it, Joe," Fisher remembers Natcher saying. "It hasn't been through the committee." . . . Wary of an amendment that had not been "processed" and convinced, he says, that the measure would actually prevent local school districts from using bilingual programs even if they wanted to (it did not), Fisher cast his vote against the Ashbrook amendment and left.

Like Joe Fisher, many congressmen say they voted against it for similar reasons. Like Joe Fisher, "most members probably didn't know what they were voting for," said an official in the Education Department's civil rights branch.[9]

This is how many representatives are forced to reach decisions on foreign and domestic policy which often involve millions of dollars—they have no exposure to the problem, are unacquainted with the facts, give no thought to possible consequences, and have little or no opportunity (as noted in chapter 4) to hear in advance from the executive branch or House leaders.

"No company could get away with such a cockeyed organization as the House of Representatives," stated the *Economist*.[10] Can one imagine a General Motors Corporation board meeting being conducted in such a fashion? Stockholders would not tolerate for a moment their directors' streaking into the board room after an issue had already been discussed, asking what it was they were voting on, and then, with little attention to relevant information, casting their ballots. And yet that is how many directors of the world's largest enterprise, the United States government, transact their business.

Foreign-Policy Votes in the House

The House, of course, is not the only institution that is, and has been, guilty of misguided approaches to international issues. The Senate and the executive branch have also been culpable. But during its foreign-policy renaissance, the House, owing largely to its quixotic methods of dealing with floor amendments and the disintegration of institutional discipline occasioned by its new-found democracy, has advanced numerous positions that have subverted our country's worldwide, regional, and bilateral aims. Let us review several of the more egregious foreign-policy errors committed in recent years by the House of Representatives, sometimes in concert with the Senate.

International Financial Institutions

FAILURE TO HONOR FUNDING COMMITMENTS

Recognizing the necessity for postwar international and financial cooperation, forty-four nations sent emissaries in July 1944 to Bretton Woods, New Hampshire, to participate in the United Nations Monetary and Financial Conference. During their one-month session the conferees drafted charters for two sister institutions (now headquartered in Washington): the International Bank for Reconstruction and Development (World Bank) and the International Monetary Fund.

On February 18, 1945, in his message to Congress accompanying his proposed Bretton Woods Arrangement Bill, President Roosevelt pointed out that "the point of history at which we stand is full of promise and change. The world will either move forward toward unity and widely shared prosperity or it will move apart in necessarily competing blocs. We have a chance, we citizens of the United States, by passing this legislation to use our influence in favor of a more united and cooperative world." [11]

This measure cleared Congress after Roosevelt's death and was signed by President Truman (PL 79-171) on July 31, 1945. The World Bank was officially launched on December 27, 1945, when its articles of agreement were signed in the State Department (now Executive Offices) building. At its inception, the principal function of the IBRD was to assist in the reconstruction of war-torn member countries. In later years the bank's primary mission has been to promote development in the globe's poorer states by providing loans from its own resources or through other lenders. To facilitate that task, it established in 1960 a subsidiary, the International Development Association (IDA), to provide low-interest credits to the world's poorest nations. During the next two decades IDA required five separate capital infusions so that it could continue its assistance programs.

In 1979 thirty-three donor nations, including the United States, agreed to a sixth replenishment amounting to $12 billion. The Carter administration pledged that the American share, $3.24 billion, would be paid in three equal installments commencing in fiscal 1981. In response to the president's request the Senate, on June 16, 1980, approved (53–24) S 2422, the International Development Banks Bill. This measure authorized our $3.24-billion contribution to IDA (although it called for only $939.6 million in fiscal 1981) and granted the United States permission to join the African Development Bank (which opened its doors to non-African membership in 1979) along with an initial $359.7-million investment in that organization.

A companion bill, HR 6811, was favorably reported by the House Committee on Banking, Finance, and Urban Affairs on May 16, 1980. Faced, however, with the certainty of embarrassing floor amendments and discouraged by a depressingly unfavorable "head count," the House leadership decided to allow HR 6811 to expire in the Rules Committee. In the absence of any authorizing legislation, the Senate Appropriations Committee then expunged the $939.6 million first installment allocation, which the House had inserted in HR Res. 644, the omnibus continuing resolution. Congress's failure to fulfill America's commitment threatened to bring IDA's lending program to an abrupt halt. Rather than permit this, several member nations provided IDA with $1.6 billion, which kept it in business at least until October 1981.

Congress's inability to enact foreign assistance appropriations bills in 1979 and 1980, relying instead on continuing resolutions, created other problems for the Carter administration. According to Secretary of State Muskie* the government was forced to operate on a scale that was one-third below project estimates. By not funding authorized commitments to international financial institutions, Muskie maintained, Congress had placed in jeopardy the right of the United States to veto prospective World Bank charter changes.[12]

Largely owing to the House's recalcitrance, the United States in 1980 was also the only major donor nation in default to multilateral lending agencies. Our total arrearage of $1.3 billion, said Treasury Secretary G. William Miller, harmed us in a variety of ways. Miller noted that at a time of turbulence and unrest in several Caribbean

---

*Muskie was nominated by President Carter on April 29, 1980, to replace Secretary Cyrus Vance, who had resigned eight days previously in protest against our military efforts to release the American hostages being held in Tehran, Iran.

and Central American countries, the Inter-American Development Bank was unable to make loans for eight months because of congressional funding delays. Miller also pointed out that "at the very time we were trying to respond to the Russian invasion of Afghanistan, our inability to come up with the U.S. share of contributions to the Asian Development Fund effectively blocked more than $250 million in loans to Pakistan. We must compete in the world not solely through military power. . . . We must compete for the minds of people who seek freedom and a better life by giving them an economic opportunity to achieve just that."[13]

America's international promises were further compromised on September 17, 1981, when the House rejected (165–226) President Reagan's first foreign-policy measure, the State Department Authorization bill for the fiscal years 1982 and 1983. (HR 3518). On this vote 131 Republicans deserted the president. Blocked by the defeat of HR 3518 was $563.8 million in contribution authority to international organizations and conferences and $367.6 million for refugee programs for fiscal year 1982. House leaders of both parties then agreed to an unusual parliamentary stratagem to resuscitate the State Department Authorization bill. On October 22 a bill (HR 4814) was introduced that was identical to the original proposal except for two changes: amendments to HR 3518, which were adopted during floor consideration, that reduced authorization figures corresponding to the executive branch's revised budget request for fiscal years 1982 and 1983. Without hearing HR 4814 in the Foreign Affairs Committee, Chairman Zablocki asked the Rules Committee to make in order his request that S 1193, the Senate-passed companion measure, be taken from the speaker's table and that its language be struck and substituted by the text of HR 4814. When this rule was adopted by voice vote on October 29, House members barred themselves from considering any other amendments. After a short debate, S 1193, as substituted by HR 4814, was passed 317–58.

COMMODITY RESTRICTIONS

On June 23, 1977, the House, by a 225–188 vote, approved an amendment to the FY 1978 Foreign Assistance Appropriations Act (HR 7797) which prohibited international financial institutions from using American contributions for the purpose of establishing or expanding the production of palm oil.* A similar reservation had been adopted by the House on April 6, 1977, as an amendment to the International Financial Institutions Authorization Bill.

The fears of American soybean producers, who strongly backed his efforts, were expressed by the amendment's sponsor, W. Henson Moore (R.-La.):

> The USDA [United States Department of Agriculture] has estimated that by 1980 one-half of the world's production of palm oil will be directly due to loans from these international institutions, with our dollars making that possible. Two-thirds of that world crop will be for export, much of it coming to this country.
>
> By 1985, Mr. Chairman, it is predicted by USDA that 15 million bushels, or one-half million acres of soybeans will not be produced, as they will be replaced by the increasing amounts of palm oil coming into this country.
>
> I ask that the committee today adopt this amendment as they did on April 6, 1977, to regain some control over our funds and to protect the American consumer and the American farmer from ourselves, for it is our money that is making this undesirable situation possible.[14]

Adoption of this amendment was a classic example of the House bowing to domestic pressures without full knowledge of the facts. The following points never emerged during the short floor debate.

First, holding back production of palm oil could have created a serious shortage of fats and oils during the 1980s. World demand for fats and oils is expected to grow faster than total supplies in the mid-1980s as incomes of the world's poorest people improve. In most developing nations consumption of fats and oils per person is far below that in economically advantaged countries. However, with the improvement of incomes in poor countries will come an increased consumption of oils. Palm oil is important to any improvement in nutrition in the Third World.

Second, the IBRD has underwritten only a negligible portion of the world's production of palm oil. According to 1977 IBRD esti-

---

*Sugar and citrus fruit also were included in the amendment but drew little comment during the June 23, 1977, floor debate.

mates, palm oil would constitute 8.7 percent of all production of fats and oils by 1980 and would increase only to 10.0 percent by 1985. Projects financed by the World Bank group were expected to account for approximately 10 percent of total palm oil output in both 1980 and 1985, or just 1 percent of the world's supply of fats and oils.

Third, despite their limited contribution to total palm oil production, IBRD's past undertakings were of significant benefit to developing countries. About 70 percent of the loans were directed to small family-operated farms. As the principal source of income for most of those families, palm oil enabled them to participate in the market economy. In Malaysia the Johore program increased rural incomes five-fold. In the Ivory Coast two schemes helped fifteen thousand small-farm families by raising individual household revenues from $350 to $1,820 annually. Many other nations, several among the world's poorest, joined the World Bank group in financing palm oil plantations. Included were Indonesia, Papua and New Guinea, Dahomey, Sierra Leone, Cameroon, Ghana, and Nigeria. In each of these countries about half of the loan cost was met by the borrowing government itself.

Fourth, the rate of economic return on these bank investments was as high as 17 percent in West Africa and up to 20 percent in Malaysia and Indonesia. In addition to aiding plantations, the World Bank group also assisted palm oil processing industries, many of which subsequently generated income in smallholder endeavors.[15]

The Senate version of HR 7797 contained no restriction like that advanced by Congressman Moore. Meeting to settle differences between the two bills, House and Senate conferees were at first unable to decide whether the palm oil amendment should be retained. Therefore they submitted their conference report to the two chambers with this and six other items in disagreement. After the House acted to recommit the report to the conferees, a second conference was held during which the participants finally abandoned the Moore Amendment. The House then passed the conference report on October 18, 1977, by a vote of 229–195.

A reprise was played in the House the following year. On August 14, 1978, Dawson Mathis (D.-Ga.) once again proposed that international financial institutions be barred from using American contributions for loans to produce palm oil for export. The fact that

Mathis weighted down his amendment with a myriad of other products, including steel, grains, sugar, citrus crops, tobacco, and tires, caused it to sink, 143–239.

COUNTRY RESTRICTIONS

When, in the spring of 1979, it marked up HR 4473, the FY 1980 Foreign Aid Appropriations Bill, the House's Foreign Operations Subcommittee inserted a provision, subsequently approved by the full Appropriations Committee, which barred any direct, bilateral assistance to Angola, Cambodia, the Central African Empire, Cuba, Laos, and Vietnam. Administration plans were not contravened by this amendment, for no aid had been planned for those countries. However, any statute foreclosing assistance to a specific state carries the risk that conditions in that nation may change, thus necessitating the laborious task of revising the law if extension of financial help is deemed advisable. (In fact, this is exactly what did occur. In September 1979 the repressive emperor of the Central African Empire, renamed the Central African Republic, was dethroned. Cambodia experienced dreadful famine in 1979–80 owing to its war with Vietnam.)

During floor debate, the ranking minority member of the Foreign Operations Subcommittee, C. W. (Bill) Young (R.-Fla.), introduced a two-word amendment—"or indirectly"—to the section of HR 4473 that barred direct aid to Angola, Cambodia, the Central African Empire, Laos, and Vietnam. "Indirect" assistance, of course, refers to American funds used to help finance those projects administered by international establishments, such as the World Bank group and the United Nations Development Program (UNDP).

The domestic political implications of the Young amendment were obvious. As will be detailed in chapter 6, those who voted against it would appear to be giving "aid and comfort" to the enemy. For several reasons, however, such a restriction would have created chaos for the lending institutions, ultimately at our country's expense.

First, these global agencies cannot accept assessed or voluntary contributions that carry with them any limitations as to their use. For instance, the World Bank charter expressly excludes any interference in members' or recipients' affairs. To insist on this amendment, the *Washington Post* concluded, "would destroy America's participation in the World Bank. That would destroy the Bank itself."[16] UNDP financial regulation 6.5, which was endorsed by the General Assembly, the UN Economic and Social Council, and the governing council of UNDP, specifically prohibits the administrator from accepting any grant that is subject to an expressed restriction.

Second, "the Young Amendment," one conservative Midwestern Republican House member told me, "politicizes the World Bank. It goes against the very principle of the system which the United States was instrumental in creating."

Third, our own economy suffers if Congress forces international aid enterprises to curtail their operations. *Time* magazine stated that "for every $1 that the U.S. contributes to international financial institutions that give aid, the recipients spend $2 to buy goods and services in the U.S. For every $1 paid into the World Bank alone, $9.50 flows into the nation's economy in the form of procurement contracts, operations expenditures and interest payments to investors in the bank's bonds."[17] Perhaps even more important in this period of growing energy shortages, suggested the *Journal of Commerce and Commercial*, is the fact that the World Bank and its affiliates "have become important sources of new energy financing. By 1983 the World Bank group expects to be lending $1.5 billion a year, or more than 10 percent of its total lending, for oil and gas development."[18] By expanding worldwide output of energy sources, these loans should help ease the price pressures squeezing all oil and natural gas importers, including the United States.

Nevertheless, on September 5, 1979, the House adopted the Young amendment, 281–117. It then unanimously accepted John Ashbrook's (R.-Ohio) motion to add Cuba to the list of those ineligible for indirect aid. As it had done in the two previous years,* the Senate Appropriations Committee omitted the Young-Ashbrook proviso in its draft on HR 4473. The full Senate, by a slim 49–46 margin, upheld the committee during floor deliberations.

For a time the Young-Ashbrook amendments produced a stalemate between House and Senate conferees. Further deadlock was averted when World Bank President Robert McNamara promised, in a letter to Congress, that his institution would make no loans

---

*In 1977 and again in 1978 the House had adopted the Young Amendment in substantially the same form as that presented in 1979.

to Vietnam during the fiscal year 1980. McNamara's surrender prompted House conferees to withdraw their insistence on inclusion of the Young-Ashbrook wording in HR 4473. For his part, while avoiding a showdown with Congress, McNamara was censured by his executive directors for compromising the sovereignty of the World Bank.[19] Worse yet, he "was left holding an empty bag for his troubles" when Congress failed to enact HR 4473, relying, instead, upon continuing appropriations to finance our multilateral and bilateral foreign assistance commitments.[20]

The United Nations

During its consideration of the FY 1979 State, Justice, Commerce, and Judiciary Appropriations Bill (HR 12934), the Senate, on August 3, 1978, accepted a motion offered by Jesse Helms (R.-N.C.) which deleted $27,776,000 earmarked for United Nations technical-assistance programs.* This amendment also precluded the use of any United States assessed contributions† to the UN and its specialized agencies for technical-assistance purposes.

The effect of the Helms amendment was twofold. Assessed dues to UN agencies go into a common fund, and one contribution cannot be distinguished from another. Thus, placing a condition on our payments could ultimately "result in the United States becoming delinquent in its regular budget contributions to the United Nations and its specialized agencies."[21] Moreover, the $27,776,000 appropriations cut also threatened to curtail or eliminate such programs as World Health Organization projects to fight smallpox and leprosy and monitor influenza and malaria outbreaks, Food and Agriculture Organization research on plant and animal diseases, International Atomic Energy Agency efforts to prevent the diversion of nuclear materials from peaceful to military uses, and the World Meteorological Organization's Weatherwatch, which supplies invaluable information to United States weather forecasters.[22]

---

*Technical assistance involves the transfer of expertise rather than the transfer of goods or capital.

†An assessed contribution honors a treaty obligation entered into by UN member states and is binding upon them. A voluntary contribution is just that, a donation made at the discretion of the member nation.

When, on September 29, 1978, the HR 12934 conference report came before the House, Representative John H. Rousselot (R.-Cal.) offered a preferential motion calling for acceptance of the Senate's restrictive language. It was adopted by voice vote without a single word of debate.

Neal Smith (D.-Iowa) then moved to restore the $27,776,000 in technical-assistance funds which had been contained in the House's original version of HR 12934 but which had been eliminated by the Senate. The House voted 143–191 to reject Smith's rescue mission. During the brief discussion of Smith's preferential motion, Congressman Rousselot stated the case for the Helms Amendment protagonists: "I believe technical assistance funds should be viewed as foreign aid and be provided for through the foreign assistance authorization and appropriations bills. I believe that we should not pay for these programs by means of our mandatory assessed share of the United Nations budget, the use of which we exercise little control over."[23]

The reaction to the House's approval of the Helms Amendment was instantaneous and worldwide. In signing HR 12934, President Carter made it clear that he strongly disapproved of the provision which,

> if allowed to stand . . . would cause the United States to violate its treaty obligations to support the organizations of the United Nations system. Withholding of, or assigning conditions to, U.S. contributions to assessed budgets of the organizations would make it virtually impossible for the organizations to accept such contributions, would seriously impair their financial and political viability and is contrary to the policy of collective financial responsibility continuously advocated by this government since the establishment of the United Nations system.
>
> This precedent would also weaken the ability of organizations of the United Nations to withstand efforts by other governments to impede their effective work. The United States has consistently opposed the Soviet Union's withholding of its assessed contributions to those programs of the United Nations which the Soviet Union has found politically unpalatable. Our efforts to stem such politicization of organizations

of the United Nations would be severely weakened if the action of the Congress is allowed to stand.[24]

The *Chattanooga Times* editorial of October 23, 1978, was typical of the American press's criticism of the Helms Amendment:
"The fact remains . . . that the U.S. is still very much a world power.
Because of that, it makes no sense whatsoever for the Congress to
let petulance override good sense and use the power of the purse
to abdicate our leadership role in the U.N."[25]

On November 17, 1978, Secretary-General Kurt Waldheim released a statement agreed to by the UN's Administrative Committee
on Coordination (ACC) at its seventy-fourth session. The ACC memorandum pointed out that

> Member States do not have the right to designate those parts
> of the regular budget or programme which are to be, or are
> not to be financed by their assessed contributions, and the
> secretaries do not have the right to earmark assessed contri-
> butions in such a manner as to prevent their being used to
> finance any specific activity or programme. . . .
>
> If allowed to persist [earmarking or withholding of assessed
> contributions] will inevitably weaken the legal foundations of
> the international organizations and jeopardize the very exis-
> tence of international cooperation within the United Nations
> system. It also constitutes an immediate threat to the financial
> viability of the United Nations system.[26]

Dispatches to the State Department by our delegation to the
United Nations indicated that in corridor conversations* delegates
from emerging nations considered the Helms Amendment a radical
alteration in American support for the development of Third World
countries.[27] In a November 20, 1978, debate in the General Assembly's Fifth Committee, India's representative, Shanti Kothari, de-
plored "attempts in recent years to confine the regular budget to
the financing of certain types of activities." Kothari expressed the
hope that the Congress would reverse its position of restraining the

---

* One of the great advantages of the United Nations General Assembly is that it permits private discussion, often at tea and coffee time in the Delegates Lounge, during
which national views can be exchanged without the necessity of formal intergovern-
mental communiques, which, once written, are difficult to retract.

United States government from financing the technical-cooperation activities of UN organizations through its assessed contributions.[28]

In 1979 the Helms ban made it impossible for the administration to release any of our $500-million contribution to the United Nations, since President Carter could not certify that these funds would not be used to finance technical-assistance activities. The House, therefore, repudiated its 1978 stand by resisting efforts to insert similar strictures in the 1979 State Department and Foreign Assistance Authorization measures. The Senate did likewise, thus permitting our country to resume the United Nations treaty guarantees that we had assumed in 1945.

Turkish Arms Ban

Cyprus lies in the eastern Mediterranean Basin approximately sixty miles south of Turkey. The island's inhabitants (Cypriots) are descended from two ethnic strains, Greek and Turkish. In 1970 Greek Cypriots accounted for 77 percent of Cyprus's 650,000 population, while Turkish Cypriots made up 18 percent.

Great Britain occupied Cyprus in 1878, established military bases there, and formally annexed it in November 1914 when neighboring Turkey allied itself with Germany in World War I. Cyprus remained a crown colony through World War II, but by the mid-1950s Greek Cypriots were becoming increasingly violent in their demands for *enosis*, union with Greece. Civilian disorder on the island eventually led to negotiations between the Greek and Turkish governments that culminated in a February 1959 conference in Zurich. The understanding reached at this meeting, which England immediately accepted, called for the independence of Cyprus under a constitution for which Greece, Turkey, and Great Britain would serve as guarantors. As finally approved, this document provided for a Greek Cypriot president, a Turkish Cypriot vice-president, and a fifty-member House of Representatives, 70 percent to be elected from the Greek and 30 percent from the Turkish communities. Cyprus became a republic in August 1960 and selected Archbishop Makarios III, patriarch of the Orthodox Church, as its first president.

Self-rule, unfortunately, did not end communal strife in Cyprus. Turmoil continued. The climax came on July 15, 1974, when the

Cypriot National Guard, led by Greek officers, deposed President Makarios. The rebels, supported by the Greek government's military junta, named Nikos Sampson, a publisher with an unsavory reputation, as the new head of state.* Acting in what it later described as its role as "guarantor," the Turkish government, on July 20, directed its armed forces to invade Cyprus. United Nations negotiators secured a cease-fire on July 22, but peace talks ended abruptly on August 14. Two hours later Turkey launched a second attack which, by August 16, had placed its forces in control of 40 percent of Cyprus's land area. By August 18 half of the Greek Cypriots residing in Turkish-occupied territory had fled.

On September 24, 1974, the House Appropriations Committee brought to the House floor a noncontroversial continuing resolution (HJRes 1131) which extended the life of those government agencies whose appropriations still had not been acted upon by Congress. This measure suddenly became the focus of heated debate when Representative Benjamin S. Rosenthal (D.-N.Y.) offered an amendment which prohibited the obligation or expenditure of funds for defense articles for use by the government of Turkey "until the President certifies to the Congress that substantial progress toward agreement has been made regarding military forces on Cyprus."

Rosenthal maintained that "quiet diplomacy" had failed to end the stalemate in Cyprus. He contended that our preagreed sales of military items to Turkey should be halted because

> U.S. arms supplied that [Turkish] invasion force. . . . The law says that all of these articles given under section 502 of the Foreign Assistance Act must be furnished solely for internal security, for legitimate self defense, or to permit the recipient country to participate in regional or collective arrangements. Then it says in section 505 (d) that if there is a violation of this, there shall be an immediate cutoff and that such country shall be immediately ineligible for further assistance. Now, the United States continues to give these arms under an ille-

---

*When civilian rule was restored in Greece on July 23, Sampson was replaced as president by Glafcos Clerides, president of the House of Representatives. To a tumultuous welcome by his followers, Archbishop Makarios returned to the island on December 7, 1974.

gal situation. . . . We ought to cut off aid to Turkey because
the law says we must.[29]

In the absence of a strong Turkish-American lobby, debate on the
Rosenthal Amendment was one-sided. The New York congressman
grudgingly conceded that it was the Greek government which "upset the apple cart to start with."[30] No mention, however, was made
of the seven hundred Greek servicemen that had been illegally stationed on Cyprus since 1967. Nor was there any reference to the
reinforcement of these soldiers in June 1974 by additional Greek
troops bearing American-made infantry weapons. There was no discussion of the threat to life and property that the Greek-led revolution posed for Turkish Cypriots. No comment was heard regarding
the frequent violations of section 504 by other American allies. The
House, in no mood to interpret the law uniformly, passed the Rosenthal Amendment overwhelmingly, 307–90.

When it approved HJRes 1131 on October 9, 1974, the Senate
retained the Rosenthal cut-off. President Ford quickly vetoed this
measure as well as HJRes 1163, which would have delayed imposition of the ban until December 10, 1974. The president finally accepted, with great reluctance, a compromise, HJRes 1167, which
permitted further aid to Turkey until December 10, provided Turkey honored the cease-fire line, neither increased nor decreased its
forces on Cyprus, and transferred no American-supplied weapons
there. Beyond December 10, Turkey would be eligible for aid only
if the president certified that substantial progress had been made
toward a military accord.

Unable to make such a certification in good conscience, President Ford halted all shipment of military items to Turkey on February 3, 1975. On July 24, 1975, the House defeated, 206–223, a
Senate-passed resolution (S 846) that would have permitted deliv-
ery to Turkey those arms for which the United States had already
been reimbursed. In a change of heart, Congress, on October 3,
1975, acted to ease the embargo. In 1977, although technically retaining the ban, both bodies approved the House Foreign Affairs
Committee's recommendation that Turkey be allowed to purchase
on credit up to $175 million worth of military supplies. Finally, on
September 12, 1978, the legislative branch removed itself from the
Cyprus dispute by granting to President Carter the authority to end

the Turkish arms embargo. Carter did so two weeks later when, in Presidential Determination Memorandum No. 78–18, he certified to Secretary Vance that "the Government of Turkey is acting in good faith to achieve a just and peaceful settlement in the Cyprus problem, the early peaceable return of refugees to their homes and properties, and continued removal of Turkish military troops from Cyprus."[31]

In his article in *Congress against the President*, Max M. Kampelman, a former legal counsel to Hubert Humphrey and one-time senior adviser to our United Nations mission, posed four critical questions regarding the House's 1974 decision to cease all military sales to Turkey: Did the House know the facts? Were sanctions applied evenly? Would the House's action produce a settlement? and Would there be counteraction by Turkey?[32]

As already seen, the first two queries can be answered in the negative. With respect to Kampelman's third question, Congressman Rosenthal was convinced that it was "in the interest of the Turkish government to get a settlement."[33] I voted for the New York solon's amendment on that very assumption, but a year later realized my mistake. During the July 24, 1975, floor debate on S 846, I confessed that "I misjudged human nature. As has so often happened in the past, a congressional threat generates a response quite opposite from that which we intended. Turkish politicians are confronted with the same pressures as we are. Thus, I should not have been surprised that national pride would preclude Turkey's giving in to congressional dictation."[34] Although negotiations continue on a sporadic basis,* Turkey has yet to cede one inch of the ground that it captured in July–August 1974.

As for Kampelman's fourth concern, retaliation, the Turkish government did it "in spades." In mid-February 1975 it withdrew its liaison officers from the United States military mission in Ankara. On July 25, 1975, the day after the House rejected S 846, Prime Minister Demirel declared that the 1969 United States–Turkish bilateral defense pact "is now dead." He ordered the closing of twenty-seven American-operated bases, including four intelligence-gathering facilities considered essential for monitoring Soviet military move-

---

*In 1977 the two sides got together under the aegis of the United Nations. The talks quickly collapsed when Turkish representatives introduced the subject of "bizonality."

ments. Tax exemptions for American servicemen were canceled. No United States military aircraft could enter Turkey without prior permission.[35] The *Washington Post* acknowledged that "far from forcing the Turks to loosen their grip . . . the embargo activated a visceral Turkish nationalism and induced Ankara to stand firm. Their aroused and wounded pride will surely make the Turks harder bargainers in any agreement struck over the American bases."[36]

So, the cessation of arms deliveries to Turkey had effects that were weakening to both sides: Turkey's military strength waned; America's operational and intelligence capacities were sapped. This, of course, disturbed European political and military leaders who feared that the congressionally ordained embargo would weaken NATO's strategic eastern flank. That concern was shared by General Lyman L. Lemnitzer, a former NATO commander who, as he departed the House gallery following the July 24, 1975, vote, exclaimed, "We've just shot ourselves in the foot!"

While not seeking to intrude openly in American internal affairs, spokesmen for our European allies privately urged legislators to repeal the Rosenthal Amendment. In the meantime, according to *Middle East* magazine, NATO countries, "doubtless with Kissinger's blessing," supplied parts to Turkey. This publication reported that "so long as . . . the two sides [Greece and Turkey] are willing to pay the market prices, there will be no shortage of arms on either side. It is likely, therefore, that the Turks will be able to preserve their margin of military advantage."[37] Additional spare parts, according to *Flight International*, were acquired by Turkey from friendly Moslem nations. "Iran is reported to have provided F-4 Phantom spares with Turkey footing the bill for that nation's [Iran's] increased orders of U.S.-supplied components."[38]

The final slap occurred in April 1978 when the chief of Russia's general staff, Marshall Nikolai Ogarkov, became the first senior Soviet military official to visit Turkey since 1933. In June, Prime Minister Ecevit (who had replaced Demirel in 1977), responding to Ogarkov's offer of military aid, traveled to Moscow to sign nonaggression, trade, and cultural agreements with the USSR.

A thaw in Turkish-American relations began when Congress, as already noted, voted on September 12, 1978, to lift the arms ban. In return Turkey permitted the United States to resume operations in the military installations that had been closed in 1975.

Africa

AMERICAN VIOLATION OF UN SANCTIONS ON RHODESIA

On December 31, 1963, the Central African Federation of Northern and Southern Rhodesia and Nyasaland was dissolved. Each of these three territories then became a separate British colony with varying degrees of self-government. Nyasaland achieved full independence in July 1964, adopting the new name Malawi. Three months later, Northern Rhodesia, renaming itself Zambia, acquired its freedom from England.

Southern Rhodesia* was another matter. It had adopted a constitution in 1961 which granted suffrage to only 5 percent of the population, mostly Europeans. In September 1964 the British government, led at the time by the Conservative party, declared that this constitution could not be the basis for independence. Prime Minister Sir Alec Douglas-Home also "made it clear that independence had to depend on the proved 'genuine desire' of the great majority of the Rhodesian population; that a referendum from the predominantly European electorate, insufficiently representing the Africans, would not suffice . . . that 'independence' could only be conceded on the basis of majority rule."[39]

When the Labour party assumed control of the House of Commons on October 16, 1964, the new prime minister, Harold Wilson, reiterated the earlier decree that "the decision to grant independence to Rhodesia rested entirely with the British Government and the Parliament which would have to be satisfied that the terms would be acceptable to the people of Southern Rhodesia as a whole."[40]

On November 11, 1965, the Unilateral Declaration of Independence (UDI) was announced by Rhodesia's prime minister, Ian Smith. Arguing that the UDI was an act of rebellion, the Wilson government asked UN member states not to recognize Rhodesian independence and to employ a voluntary economic boycott against that territory. In 1966 the Security Council, with the United States assenting, was persuaded by Wilson to impose selective economic sanctions against Rhodesia. Later that year the Security Council,

---

*Southern Rhodesia became known as Rhodesia in 1965 and ultimately adopted the African name of Zimbabwe. For the sake of consistency, I shall refer to the country as Rhodesia in the following pages.

again with American concurrence, adopted a comprehensive trade ban.

In April 1966 the United Kingdom's permanent representative to the UN, Lord Caradon, asked for a meeting of the Security Council, requesting that it recognize Rhodesia's actions as a "threat to international peace and security." On Easter eve, with the approval of the United States, the council agreed to invoke chapter 7 of the United Nations Charter. But Great Britain was unwilling to go beyond that point. Using its veto power, the United Kingdom quashed subsequent Security Council resolutions that would have authorized military action to bring Rhodesia into compliance with the UN mandate.

By 1970, as a result of the decolonization movement which had accelerated after World War II, there were forty independent states (excluding Rhodesia and South Africa) on the African continent. Whatever their political and economic philosophies, the leaders of those countries were united on one point: Africa could not be truly free until majority rule was enjoyed by all of its people. Consequently, heading the agenda of every Organization of African Unity (OAU) session was the issue of minority domination in Rhodesia, South Africa, Namibia (Southwest Africa), and the three remaining colonies on the continent, Portuguese-controlled Angola, Mozambique, and Guinea-Bissau. That concern was communicated to other international forums, such as the United Nations General Assembly and Security Council, with strong pleas for appropriate action to halt racial discrimination in those six enclaves.

In late 1971 Congress took a step which placed United States policy squarely at odds with this African sentiment, thus polarizing attitudes for the next six years. Reporting the FY 1972 Defense Procurement Authorization Bill (HR 8687), the Senate Armed Services Committee included an amendment which, in effect, ordered the president to permit the importation of Rhodesian chromium ore so as to reduce our dependence upon Russia as a supplier of that metal. Two attempts to excise this section met with defeat on the Senate floor (36–46 and 36–40). Finally, by voice vote, senators accepted an amendment to defer its implementation until January 1, 1972.

House conferees acceded to Senate demands that the chrome provision be incorporated in the HR 8687 conference report. When the report came before the House on November 10, 1971,

Donald Fraser (D.-Minn.), citing the Legislative Reorganization Act of 1970, challenged the amendment as "nongermane." Prior to the vote on Fraser's motion, Speaker Albert ruled that the rejection of any portion of the conference report would nullify the entire report. Partly because of this threat, the House voted 251–100 to retain the "UN sanction-buster," after which it gave oral approval to the entire report.

If Congress had deliberately sought to alienate Africans, it could not have improved upon its November 1971 performance. There followed outspoken criticism of America's seeming insensitivity to African hopes, criticism which accused us of a callousness that appeared to betray our own "one-man-one-vote" heritage. As one African official bluntly told a delegation of visiting congressmen: "Although the United States Government continues to support sanctions against Rhodesia, it has decided to import chrome ore from Rhodesia. This is a violation of U.N. sanctions by a major power and should, as far as Africans are concerned, raise questions about the U.S. commitment to the United Nations, to the independence movement, and to the questions of majority rule. . . . The decision to buy chrome is another evidence of U.S. support of minority rule and racial discrimination."[41]

On July 28, 1972, with the United States abstaining, the Security Council approved, 14–0, a resolution sponsored by its three African members—Guinea, Somalia, and the Sudan—which condemned "all acts violating" its embargo against Rhodesia.[42] On December 7, 1972, the UN General Assembly, by a vote of 92–8 (and 22 abstentions), castigated the United States for deliberately disregarding Rhodesian economic sanctions, which it was committed to uphold. That was the first instance in which the word *condemn* had been directed against the United States by name in an assembly resolution.[43]

In an address delivered in Addis Ababa, on December 7, 1973, Dr. Njoroge Mungai, foreign minister of Kenya,* reiterated earlier warnings that "Africa has reason to feel totally disappointed by American policies. . . . This activity [breaking of sanctions] made nonsense of American commitments to the U.N. and of her purported concern for the freedom and liberty of Africans. This gives the im-

---

* In Dr. Mungai's absence, his speech was read by the Hon. E. W. Mwangale, member of the Kenya parliament.

pression that the United States was merely using the United Nations as a cover-up to promote her own interests at the expense of Africans."[44]

Several attempts were made to repeal the statute permitting the importation of Rhodesian chrome ore. In 1975 one such proposal, the Bill to Amend the United Nations Participation Act of 1945 (HR 1287), was referred sequentially to the House Foreign Affairs and Armed Services committees. The former reported HR 1287 favorably, 17–8, while the latter rejected it, 7–29. The Rules Committee, in deference to both panels, brought HR 1287 to the House floor with the stipulation that the three-hour debate be divided equally between the two committees and the bill's chief sponsor, Representative Fraser.

During floor discussion the undesirability of our continued reliance upon the Soviet Union as a principal supplier of chrome ore was stressed by those who opposed HR 1287. Yet, it was pointed out by proponents that the National Security Council and the Department of Defense had determined that Rhodesian chrome was not vital to our country's welfare. The strategic stockpile (as of 1975) was deemed more than adequate to meet our defense needs, and excess stocks could provide the equivalent of decades of imports of Rhodesian ore.

House members were cautioned by Representative William Frenzel, a Minnesota Republican, that "a major share of the world's dwindling reserves are located on the African continent and a significant proportion of our petroleum also comes from that area. It makes good sense to try and maintain friendly relations with these resource rich countries, as long as we are not denying ourselves needed materials, and as long as the moral issue is right."[45]

John Buchanan (R.-Ala.), a Baptist minister, concluded the debate by urging the House to "join the President and Secretary of State and say that this is the way to take a stand for human rights and for self-determination and to put our country firmly down on the side of right on this matter."[46] These arguments were of no avail. HR 1287 failed, 187–209.

In 1977, following an intensive lobbying effort by President Carter, Congress finally reversed itself and reimposed the ban on Rhodesian chrome. After garnering House approval on March 14, 1977 (250–146), the Chrome Import Bill (HR 1746), cleared the Senate the next day by a 66–26 margin.

HOUSE INVOLVEMENT IN PEACE NEGOTIATIONS IN RHODESIA

Debilitated by the costly struggle to maintain control over its African colonies, the government of Portugal, in April 1974, proclaimed its intention to grant independence to Angola, Mozambique, and Guinea-Bissau. Transition to home rule proceeded relatively smoothly in Mozambique and Guinea-Bissau. However, with three political parties contesting for control in Angola, its independence day—November 11, 1975—was celebrated in the midst of a civil war. Aided by three thousand Cuban troops, Agostino Neto was ultimately able to establish a government in Luanda, the former colonial capital. With the continued support of Castro's forces, Neto's successor, Eduardo Dos Santos, still retained the reins of power in Angola in 1981.*

In April 1976, Secretary Kissinger, concerned by Communist gains on the African continent, visited southern Africa to reaffirm, as President Ford put it, "this country's belief in the right of self-determination of any country, including the United States—that, of course, is how we became a country—and, secondly, that under any and all circumstances this country stands for full protection of minority rights."[47]

Speaking on the campus of his alma mater, the University of Michigan, on September 15, 1976, Ford summarized his "comprehensive, affirmative African policy" which was formulated "to help all the parties, black and white, involved in the mounting crisis in southern Africa, to find a peaceful and just solution to their many and

---

* Congress learned in December 1975 that the CIA was assisting anti-Communist factions in Angola. In addition, the United States government funneled $32 million in "contingency funds" to Angola guerrilla forces supported by the government of South Africa. Fearing another "Vietnam quagmire" and concerned about the enmity in black Africa which our alliance with South Africa would incur, the Senate (on December 19, 1975) and the House (on January 27, 1976) approved Senator John Tunney's (D.-Cal.) amendment to the Defense Appropriations Bill which prohibited the use of any funds "for any activities involving Angola directly or indirectly."

While I agreed at the time that it was not in our national interest to involve ourselves in Angola's internal affairs, in retrospect I question the wisdom of strapping the executive branch with a statutory restriction foreclosing its freedom to maneuver. In 1980 conferees modified and then accepted a Senate-approved amendment to the FY 1981 Foreign Aid Authorization Bill (HR 6442) which continued the prohibition of aid to any faction for military or covert operations in Angola unless waived by passage of a joint resolution.

complex differences. . . . In particular, we are working in close collaboration with the United Kingdom which has historical and legal responsibility in Rhodesia."[48]

The Ford-Kissinger initiative was perpetuated by President Carter and Secretary Vance. In 1977, UN Ambassador Andrew Young and England's foreign minister, Dr. David Owen, developed the so-called British-American Plan, by which they hoped to achieve a peaceful transition to majority rule in Rhodesia. The proposal, backed by the presidents of the "front-line states,"* called for an "all-parties conference" to which would be invited representatives of each of the disparate groups in Rhodesia—the Smith white minority government, the African National Council (a conglomerate of black national factions headed by Bishop Abel Muzorewa), and the Patriotic Front (whose leaders, Joshua Nkomo and Robert Mugabe, and their forty thousand guerrilla fighters operated from bases outside the country).

Ian Smith, however, moved quickly to sidetrack the plan. On March 3, 1978, an "internal settlement" was reached between Smith and three black leaders, Bishop Muzorewa, Ndabaningi Sithole, and Chief Jeremiah Chirau, which called for a new constitution and parliamentary elections (scheduled for December 31, 1978) in which all Rhodesians eighteen years of age and older could vote. The constitution effectively preserved white political supremacy, however. Key cabinet posts were reserved for Smith's followers, who also were guaranteed 28 percent of the seats in the new parliament, thereby giving them veto power over any future constitutional amendment proposals.

This internal settlement did not meet the British-American criteria, for excluded from the deliberations leading to its adoption was the Patriotic Front, which claimed to represent a significant portion of Rhodesia's population. For this reason President Carter, Prime Minister James Callaghan, and the front-line presidents denounced the pact. Civil strife grew with the Patriotic Front stepping up its border incursions and the Rhodesian army retaliating with strikes against guerrilla camps in Zambia and Mozambique. In the absence of an agreement involving all elements of Rhodesian society, it was

---

*The "front-line states" are those five countries which abut Rhodesia—Mozambique, Zambia, Angola, Tanzania, and Botswana.

clear that the war would escalate further. Thus Young and Owen continued to press Smith, the three black members of the internal settlement's Council of Ministers, the Patriotic Front, and the front-line presidents to agree to an all-parties conference.

On August 2, 1978, while considering the International Security Assistance Authorization Bill (HR 12514), the House again became enmeshed in the complicated Rhodesian tangle. By adopting, 229–180, an amendment introduced by Representative Ichord the House agreed to prohibit the enforcement of UN sanctions against Rhodesia after December 31, 1978, unless the president determined that a government had not been installed that was chosen by free elections in which all political groups were allowed to participate.

Ichord insisted that his proposal did not interfere with the right of the president to conduct foreign policy. Rather, the Missouri congressman argued, his amendment simply did "not require the present Smith-Sithole-Muzorewa government to negotiate with the communist-backed, admittedly backed by the Soviet Union and Cuba, faction trying to shoot itself into power in Rhodesia."[49] Obviously, by not including the Patriotic Front in his interpretation of "all political groups," Ichord was challenging President Carter to explain, after Rhodesia's elections, why its government had not been chosen in a "free election."

It is difficult to ascribe motives to the 220 House members who voted to intrude Congress into the delicate Rhodesian negotiations. It was a "no-win" proposition—no funds were allocated to Rhodesia in HR 12514, and lifting the embargo would have had little, if any, impact on our economy. But there was much to lose.

First, the United States, by ending sanctions, would have again transgressed a Security Council decision that it had pledged to honor. Furthermore, unilateral termination of the Rhodesian embargo would have further strained America's relations with African nations. In fact, on July 22, 1978, the OAU, at its annual summit meeting in Khartoum, Sudan, passed an "urgent resolution" which warned that any breach of UN economic sanctions against Rhodesia would be regarded as "an unfriendly act" and a "particular affront to the dignity and aspirations" of the African people.[50]

Finally, although the covening of an all-parties conference was by no means a certainty, the premature recognition by the House of a government formed without full citizen participation would have run the risk of prolonging hostilities in Rhodesia. That, in turn, might have led, as it did in Angola, to the introduction of arms by non-African powers, a possibility that both the Congress and the president hoped to avoid.

The Ichord Amendment was softened by House-Senate conferees, thus making it more acceptable to President Carter, who thereupon signed HR 12514. As the elections scheduled for December 1978 eventually were postponed, Ichord's deadline became moot.

The elections prescribed in the internal settlement were held in April 1979, and Muzorewa was installed as prime minister. However, confronted with the prospect of a long struggle and the attendant increase in casualties and further economic decline, Muzorewa and Smith agreed in September 1979 to meet with representatives of the Patriotic Front at Lancaster House, London. Prodded by Lord Carrington* (who received considerable support from the front-line presidents, who were anxious for a settlement), both sides finally accepted a new constitution and agreed to replace Muzorewa with a British governor and administrators who would guide the country until new national elections could be held. On December 12, 1979, Rhodesia resumed its former status as a British colony when Lord Soames became its interim governor. The next day, the United Kingdom terminated its economic embargo, and Soames ordered an end to Rhodesian army raids on guerrilla camps in neighboring nations. On December 16, President Carter lifted United States sanctions. A cease-fire agreement was signed on December 21 and took effect on December 28. New elections, held on February 27–29, 1980, produced a resounding victory for Robert Mugabe, one of the partners in the Patriotic Front movement. At formal ceremonies on April 18, 1980, the Union Jack was lowered for the last time and the new flag of Zimbabwe was hoisted in its place.

On April 14, 1980, the State Department announced its intention to grant the new nation $20 million in assistance during fiscal 1980 and another $25–30 million the following year. This request was then approved by both the House and Senate, subject to a presidential report every sixty days apprising the Congress of Prime Minister Mugabe's progress in instituting the Declaration of Rights contained in the Lancaster House compact.

---

*Carrington replaced Dr. Owen as foreign minister when the Conservative party won a majority of seats in Britain's 1979 parliamentary elections.

ZAMBIA

Zambia, a landlocked country in central southern Africa, is situated on the northern border of Rhodesia. With a population of 5.35 million and an annual per capita gross national product of $415, Zambia is among the world's least developed nations.[51] Until the late 1970s most of its limited governmental revenues, which were gained largely through the sale of copper, were devoted to education and rural development.

On January 17, 1972, Dr. K. D. Kaunda, president of the Republic of Zambia, addressed the opening session of the Conference of African and American Representatives in Lusaka's Malungushi Hall. Kaunda stated that Africans "cannot allow our countries to be the battleground for competing ideologies. We have only one ideology—the ideology of peace and development." But Kaunda assured his audience that "there is every reason why we should increase our cooperation with the United States. Our ties are deeply rooted in history, through the presence in that continent of millions of the descendants of Africans with whom we have unbreakable bonds of affinity."[52]

In the years following that conference Zambia gave tangible evidence of its friendship for America. President Kaunda's cooperation was critical to the success of British-American efforts to achieve a peaceful transition to majority rule in Rhodesia. He remained a principal figure in UN Ambassador Donald McHenry's* plan to settle the conflict in Namibia (Southwest Africa). Zambia's delegate to the UN General Assembly voted in favor of the American resolution to condemn the taking of hostages in Iran, and President Kaunda publicly criticized Russia's December 1979 invasion of Afghanistan.

In 1979 Zambia was the target of air and ground attacks launched initially from Rhodesia and later from South Africa. To protect his country from further encroachments, President Kaunda asked the United States for arms, but our government refused his request on the grounds that Zambia did not need additional military equipment. Kaunda next turned to Great Britain and met the same response. After also being rejected by the West German government, Kaunda, in desperation, approached the Soviets, who agreed to sup-

---

*McHenry replaced Andrew Young as our permanent representative to the United Nations on September 21, 1979.

ply Zambia with MIG-21 aircraft. The terms called for cash payments over a ten-year span.

For fiscal 1981, the Carter administration asked Congress for $27 million for Zambia, a $3-million reduction from the previous year's request. During the March 25, 1980, Foreign Affairs Committee mark-up of the Foreign Assistance Authorization Bill (HR 6942), Millicent Fenwick (R.-N.J.) sought to delete $7 million of the $27 million earmarked for Zambia because "it seem[ed] preposterous to take money out of our people's pockets to give to development programs for people who have that kind of cash for war supplies."[53] Fenwick's amendment lost 6 to 11 in committee, but she was more successful on the House floor, where her proposal (offered on June 5, 1980) carried 220–148.

By no means could this have been construed as a major foreign-policy setback for the executive branch. Nevertheless, Representative Fenwick's gesture seemed a gratuitous slap at a friendly non-aligned state whose support is crucial to the United States in an area of the world where we are actively competing for influence. In an August 1980 conversation in New York with a Foreign Affairs Committee staff consultant, a high-ranking Zambian official expressed displeasure but did not seem disconsolate about the House's action. While he found it difficult to understand why Zambia's request for arms was denied by another English-speaking democracy, he was even more puzzled why his country was then punished for going elsewhere for its needs. Evidently the Senate agreed, for during consideration of HR 6942 it deleted the Zambian restriction. Nor was the Fenwick Amendment restored in the conference report. However, in their joint explanatory statement of the Committee of Conference, conferees recommended that only $20.3 million be given Zambia, although discretionary powers were granted to the State Department to increase that sum in its overall allocation of $102.3 million to southern Africa.

Latin America

On September 21, 1973, Henry Kissinger was confirmed as secretary of state, replacing William P. Rogers who had just resigned that post. Among the new secretary's priorities was his desire to repair our relations with Latin America, long neglected during our preoccupation with Southeast Asia.

In October, while attending a UN General Assembly session in New York, Kissinger invited the Western Hemisphere foreign ministers and ambassadors with whom he met to join in a "new dialogue" on inter-American issues. The response to the secretary's proposal was positive. Colombia convoked the Conference of Foreign Ministers of Latin America for Continental Cooperation in Bogota on November 14–16, 1973, during which the delegates adopted an eight-point agenda for further discussion with the United States. Heading the negotiating list were the issues of cooperation for development and the future of the Panama Canal.

The Bogota document served as the basis for the Tlateloloco Conference held in Mexico City, February 18–23, 1974. Secretary Kissinger and his twenty-four hemisphere counterparts went over the eight Bogota items topic by topic and on February 23 reached a series of agreements which were outlined in the Declaration of Tlateloloco.

In the declaration the United States offered to promote the integrated development of the region by enacting a system of generalized trade preferences. The conferees also expressed in the declaration their approbation of the February 7 concord between the United States and Panama as "a significant step forward on the road to a definitive solution of the Panama Canal question."[54] At its conclusion, Secretary Kissinger hailed the conference as the start of "a new relationship between the United States and Latin America and the Caribbean."[55] At the time, Kissinger could not have foreseen that Congress would make this "new relationship" less than harmonious.

EXCLUSION OF VENEZUELA AND ECUADOR
FROM GENERAL TRADE PREFERENCES

In February 1972 the United States, the European Community, and Japan agreed to "initiate and actively support multilateral and comprehensive negotiations in the framework of GATT [General Agreement on Tariffs and Trade] beginning in 1973 . . . with a view to the expansion and greater liberalization of world trade . . . on the basis of mutual advantage and mutual commitment with overall reciprocity."[56] On April 10, 1973, President Nixon submitted to Congress a special message calling for a five-year renewal of presidential authority (which had expired on June 30, 1967) to enter into new exchange arrangements with our trading partners. Nixon specifically asked that the United States be permitted "to join with other developed countries in helping to improve the access of poorer nations to the markets of developed countries. Under this arrangement certain products of developing nations would benefit from preferential treatment for a ten-year period, creating new export opportunities for such countries."[57]

On December 11, 1973, the House passed, 272–140, the Trade Reform Bill (HR 10710), which granted the executive branch the right, in conjunction with other GATT members, to harmonize, reduce, or eliminate tariff and nontariff barriers.* HR 10710 also extended, but on a somewhat more limited scale than that asked by President Nixon, general tariff preferences to developing countries.

Before the Senate could act on the Trade Reform Bill, Arab members of the Organization of Petroleum Exporting Countries (OPEC) imposed a five-month embargo (October 18, 1973–March 18, 1974) on oil shipments to the United States and other nations considered to be pursuing pro-Israeli policies. During that same period the price of oil imported by the United States shot up 400 percent.

An angry Senate Finance Committee amended HR 10710 by denying tariff preferences to members of OPEC or any other cartels that withheld supplies or raised the price of a commodity to "unreasonable" levels. This exclusion was retained by the full Senate when it approved HR 10710 on December 13, 1974 (77–4), and was accepted by House conferees six days later.

The House considered and approved, 323–36, the HR 10710 conference report on the last day of the Ninety-third Congress (December 20, 1974). During consideration of the conference report no question was raised by members regarding the fairness of punishing those nations, especially our friends to the south, which had continued to supply oil to the United States throughout the Arab embargo. If the House was blind to this inequity, officials in Latin America were not.

Writing in the *Foreign Service Journal*, Robert Pastor observed that the OPEC exclusion "provoked a rare unanimous condemnation from the Latin and Caribbean governments . . . and a prema-

---

* Nontariff barriers include such obstructions to international trade as import quotas, export subsidies, and preferential government procurement policies.

ture muting, if not silencing, of the 'new dialogue.'"[58] In early January 1975, for example, President Pérez of Venezuela accused the United States of "an obvious act of economic aggression and pressure" which he felt threatened his country's policy of "defending our raw materials and basic products."[59] In letters to the presidents of Venezuela and Ecuador, President Velasco of Peru attacked the trade act's provisions as "coercive and discriminatory measures which seriously threaten the integral development of Latin America and Third World countries."[60]

At a special meeting, held on January 23, 1975, twenty members of the permanent council of the Organization of American States (OAS) adopted a resolution citing the trade act as discriminatory and coercive and in contravention of the principles laid down in the Charter of Economic Rights and Duties of States approved by the UN General Assembly in December 1974.

On January 20, 1975, Argentina notified Washington and twenty-two other Western Hemisphere governments that, as host country, it had decided to postpone indefinitely a conference of foreign ministers set for Buenos Aires in March. According to the Argentine Foreign Office, the decision had been made because the trade act's "rigidity and lack of equity" harmed fundamental interests of Latin American countries.[61]

Bitterness permeated the OAS General Assembly sessions of May 5–19, 1975, in Washington, with the Venezuelan and Ecuadorian representatives leading the protests against the United States decision to withhold trade preferences from all OPEC-member nations. The debate shifted to the White House's state dining room on September 25, 1975, when Colombia's president, Alfonso Lopez Michelson, stated in his toast that "from a Latin American point of view, the new Trade Act of the United States is not without shortcomings, among other reasons, because of the discriminatory treatment given to Ecuador and Venezuela."[62]

As a result of Congress's refusal in 1975 to heed President Ford's recommendation that it "reconsider one provision of the 1974 trade act which had had an unfortunate and unintended impact on our relations with Latin America,"[63] this issue became a permanent item on OAS agendas. In June 1976 the OAS General Assembly approved another resolution criticizing the act's discriminatory trade preference clause, and the matter was brought up again by Latin American delegations at each subsequent session of that body.

Thus, much to the embarrassment of presidents Ford and Carter, the controversy simmered for another three years.

Latin American feelings were finally soothed on July 26, 1979, when Congress cleared the Trade Agreements Act of 1979 (HR 4537)* for White House approval. Section 1111 of this measure permitted the extension of trade preferences to any OPEC country that had entered into a bilateral product trade agreement with the United States prior to January 3, 1980. Utilizing section 1111, President Carter designated Ecuador and Venezuela as "beneficial developing countries" eligible for general trade preferences, thereby redeeming, six years and many disputes later, the Kissinger pledge made at Tlateloloco in 1973. The OAS permanent council, in turn, removed the trade act from its permanent agenda.

HOUSE PROHIBITION OF TREATY NEGOTIATIONS WITH PANAMA

From the time the American-operated ninety-five-ton Bucyrus steam shovel scooped its first load of earth from the Culebra Cut on November 16, 1904, the Panama Canal infected inter-American unity. The Republic of Panama considered the Hay-Bunau-Varilla Treaty of 1903 a violation of its sovereignty, a sentiment shared by most other Western Hemisphere and Third World nations. Yet many in the United States argued that since our country built and paid for the canal, we should not yield to Panama's entreaties. The nadir in our relations with Panama was reached on January 9, 1964, when riots claimed four American and twenty-one Panamanian lives. The following day Panama severed diplomatic relations with the United States.

Acting as conciliator, the general committee of the OAS ultimately persuaded the two countries to resume formal contacts. In proclaiming this breakthrough on April 3, 1964, the chairman of the general committee also announced that Panama and the United States "would designate without delay Special Ambassadors with sufficient powers to seek the prompt elimination of the causes of conflict [status of the Panama Canal] between the two countries."[64]

President Johnson appointed former secretary of the Treasury Robert B. Anderson as his special ambassador, and by June 1967 ne-

---

* HR 4537 provided for statutory implementation of the nontariff agreements adopted by GATT negotiators earlier in the year.

gotiators had completed drafts of three separate canal treaties. However, the premature release of their contents caused widespread disgruntlement, especially in Panama, and led the government of Panama to repudiate the treaties in 1968.

Talks were resumed in 1970, and in September 1973, following Secretary Kissinger's promising of a "new dialogue," President Nixon appointed Ambassador Ellsworth Bunker as chief negotiator in Panama. On February 7, 1974, Secretary Kissinger and Juan Antonio Tack, minister of foreign affairs for Panama, initiated a joint statement of principles (which, as already noted, was applauded in the Declaration of Tlateloloco) for the negotiation of a new Panama Canal treaty. Kissinger proudly referred to this statement as "a new era in the history of our hemisphere [which] makes a major contribution to the structure of world peace."[65]

Sixteen months later the House of Representatives decided that the canal negotiations should end. Anxious to get an early start on the twelve-day Independence Day recess set to commence that afternoon (June 26, 1975), House leaders scheduled for floor disposition a noncontroversial bill, the State, Justice, Commerce, the Judiciary, and Related Agencies Appropriations for fiscal 1976 (HR 8121). What followed was anything but placid.

During the five-minute rule, Gene Snyder (R.-Ky.) offered an amendment to the State Department section of HR 8121 which forbade the expenditure of any funds "appropriated in this title . . . for the purpose of negotiating the surrender or relinquishment of any U.S. rights in the Panama Canal Zone." Snyder defended his proposal on the grounds that it carried "the outspoken support of the overwhelming mass of the people. . . . They stand for maintaining our complete control over that vital waterway and the 10-mile strip through which it passes."

Congressman Dante Fascell (D.-Fla.), chairman of the House Foreign Affairs Inter-American Subcommittee, argued that adoption of the Snyder Amendment would "destroy U.S. credibility throughout Latin America." Elford Cederberg, ranking Republican on the Appropriations Committee, stated that, while he shared Snyder's position, "I do not see how we can deny the President, any President, his constitutional right of negotiation." But oblivious to the constitutional and foreign-policy implications of the Snyder Amendment, the House adopted it 246–164.[66]

While House members participated in parades celebrating the

anniversary of our own revolution, the Snyder Amendment triggered in Central America a reaction somewhat akin to our "Spirit of
'76." Hints of a popular uprising were heard. In Mexico demonstra-
tions protested the House's action. The adviser to Panama's Foreign
Ministry commented that "nobody can prevent the Panamanians
from destroying, paralyzing or putting the canal out of commission."[67] In a news column, Mario Augusto Opina reminded readers
that "U.S. presence in Panama cannot continue without the Panamanian people's consent, and the American people would not be
able to withstand a confrontation with Panama in Panamanian
territory."[68]

Taking into account the Snyder Amendment's unfavorable recep-
tion abroad, the Senate dropped it from its version of HR 8121.
House-Senate conferees then agreed to a "sense-of-the-Congress"
substitute for the restrictive Snyder language—"It is the sense of
Congress that any new treaty or agreement must protect the vital
interests of the U.S. in the operation, maintenance, property and defense of the Canal." Considering this a dissimulation, the House rejected the conference phraseology, 197–203, on September 24,
1975.

After news of this vote reached Panama City, six to eight hundred
rock-throwing youths attacked the American Embassy, breaking
over a hundred windows. No Americans were injured, but several
Panamanian National Guardsmen were hurt when they sought to
disperse the demonstrators.[69]

Conferees adopted a second report, adding five words to the original verbiage—"in the Canal Zone and" (inserted between "U.S."
and "in"). Thanks to an all-out selling effort by President Ford's
forces on the Hill, this nonenforceable compromise was accepted
by the House, 212–201, on September 26. Ambassador Bunker
was free to continue to employ his considerable skills in Panama.

HOUSE DEFEAT OF THE CANAL TREATY
IMPLEMENTATION CONFERENCE REPORT

On February 8, 1977, President Carter added a new recruit to
the canal treaty negotiating team when he nominated Sol M. Linowitz (who, like Bunker, was a business executive turned diplomat)
as special representative to the president with the personal rank of
ambassador. By August 12, 1977, Carter was able to announce that
Bunker and Linowitz had reached an agreement in principle with

Panamanian representatives. As described by the president, the proposed treaty would permit the United States to

> have operating control and the right to protect and defend the Panama Canal with our own military forces until the end of this century.* . . . Under a separate neutrality treaty, we will have the right to assure the maintenance of the permanent neutrality of the canal as we may deem necessary. Our own warships are guaranteed the permanent right to expeditious passage without regard to their type of propulsion or the cargo they carry. . . . We will work with Panama to assess the need for a sea-level canal and will also cooperate on possible improvements to the existing canal.
>
> I believe that these treaties will help to usher in a new day in hemispheric relations.[70]

On September 7, 1977, in the presence of twenty-six other Western Hemisphere heads of state, President Carter and General Omar Torrijos signed the two treaties in Washington's Pan American Union Building (headquarters of the OAS). In his remarks during the signing ceremonies, the president referred to the treaties as a "bipartisan effort . . . which testifies to the maturity and the good judgment and the decency of our people."[71]

By a better than two-to-one majority, Panamanian citizens approved the treaties in an October 23, 1977, plebiscite. For Jimmy Carter, treaty ratification did not come quite as easily. The Senate debated the two treaties for ten weeks, during which time there were offered 145 amendments, twenty-six reservations, eighteen understandings, and three declarations.[72] Those changes that were adopted, although controversial in some instances, did no particular violence to the treaties.

On March 16, 1978, in an electrically charged scene worthy of a Hollywood production, the Senate approved the neutrality treaty with one vote to spare, 68–32 (many of us from the House lined the walls of the Senate chamber while the roll was called). The vote on the basic treaty on April 18, although less dramatic, still resulted in a narrow win (again, 68–32) for treaty supporters.

---

*For perhaps obvious reasons, Carter did not specifically allude to the fact that on January 1, 2000, Panama would assume full responsibility for administering, operating, and securing the canal.

It was agreed that October 1, 1979, would be the effective date of the treaties. This would give Congress sufficient time to enact the statutes necessary to carry out the provisions of the 1977 conventions. Specifically, legislation was required to: authorize the transfer of the former Canal Zone to the Republic of Panama on October 1, 1979; establish procedures describing the property to be transferred; create the Panama Canal Commission, which would oversee the waterway's operations through the end of the century; develop toll, investment interest, and other financial standards; provide for protection of employment rights of American personnel; and permit immigration to the United States of past and present employees (and their families) of the Panama Canal Company.

The House sidetracked the administration's legislative proposal in favor of one (HR 111) sponsored by John Murphy, chairman of the Merchant Marine and Fisheries Committee. Although, in the view of Panamanian President Royo, Murphy's bill "did not harmonize with the letter and spirit of the Carter-Torrijos treaties," it was approved by the House, 224–202, on June 21, 1979.[73]

Clinging to the principle that the bill implementing the treaties should conform to the treaties' mandates, the Senate Armed Services Committee substantially revised HR 111. After defeating several attempts to restore portions of the original Murphy language, the Senate finally approved the Armed Services bill, 64–30, on July 26.

House and Senate conferees fashioned a compromise, which was reported to both bodies on September 17, 1979, a mere fourteen days before the treaties were to become operative. While yielding to House demands that canal operations be subject to annual authorizations and appropriations, conferees did agree to eliminate the other House-approved features that the administration and the Senate considered violative of the treaties.

The Senate adopted the conference report, 60–35, on September 20. Four hours later the HR 111 conference report was derailed by the House of Representatives, 192–203. In rejecting the report, House members chose to ignore Edward Derwinski's (R.-Ill.) remonstrance: "Before you vote against the conference report, please think of the consequences. The consequences could be catastrophic to the ability of our people that operate the canal and it will be catastrophic to the image of the United States throughout Latin America." Instead, they were moved by George Hansen's rhetorical questions:

Does it bother you to have Soviet combat troops in Cuba? Does it bother you to have Castro and Torrijos spreading Marxist terrorism around the Caribbean? [Although a dictator, Torrijos was not a Communist.] Does it bother you to have Soviet and Cuban troops standing between us and 75 percent of our oil imports? Does it bother you to have: first, billions paid to Panama to take the canal; and second, treaty guarantees broken, jeopardizing United States control of the canal over the next 20 years?[74]

Obviously, 203 House members *were* "bothered."

President Royo left no doubt as to where he stood on the issue of effecting the provisions of the treaty in the absence of implementing legislation. "As of October 1, we will begin exercising all those governmental and jurisdictional powers that Panama is entitled to. . . . It will not be the government that is going to or wants to enter the Canal Zone. . . . The Panamanian people, rather than a government or party, are going to enter the Canal Zone."[75]

The next day (September 22) Panama's Foreign Minister Ozores made it clear that "Panama will demand fulfillment of that which has been signed and ratified with the U.S. because the approval or rejection of laws for implementation constitutes a U.S. internal problem."[76] The Panamanian government went ahead with its October 1 celebration plans. The presidents of Peru and Bolivia confirmed that they would be present at the transfer ceremonies.[77]

The crisis was averted, however, when, on September 24, House conferees agreed to a new report after wrangling several minor concessions from their Senate colleagues. When the second conference report reached the House floor on September 26 (the Senate had approved it, 63–32, a day earlier), HR 111's chief critic, Robert Bauman (R.-Md.), admitted that "today we are at the end of the road. . . . For the continued operation of this canal we need in place some implementing legislation and this is the only implementing legislation left. We do not really have time to rewrite it."[78] Taking Bauman at his word, twenty-five of his followers reversed their earlier vote, thereby ensuring House passage of the second conference report, 232–188.

Five days later, with Vice-President Walter Mondale in attendance, Panama celebrated the reversion of the Canal Zone to its jurisdiction. "A state within a state no longer exists" declared President Royo.[79] Another promise, made at Tlateloloco, finally had been fulfilled.

The Middle East—Syria

When the House, on June 5, 1980, vented its wrath upon Syria, no notice of it appeared in the two leading newspapers in Damascus, *Al-Thawara* and *Tishrin*. Instead, the leaders of that nation reacted with unspoken relief. When asked about the House's decision to eliminate all funds ($3.5 million) for his country contained in the FY 1981 Foreign Aid Authorization Bill, one Syrian official privately expressed the view that "ending the abuse which we annually receive from Congress will more than compensate us for the money which we will lose. As you know, we never requested American assistance—this was an initiative of the United States government. Unfortunately, the foreign aid bill is used each year by some congressmen as a means of attacking Syria. So for us, eliminating this appropriation was no 'big deal.'"

Following the Yom Kippur War in 1973, Syria was regarded by three successive American administrations as an indispensable element in any comprehensive Middle East peace accord. That nation's central, strategic location, bordering Lebanon, Iraq, Jordan, and Israel, requires its participation in the settlement process. From the point of view of the United States, Syria's role as a peacemaker would be compromised if that state became unduly dependent upon Russia or joined the radical Arab bloc. Thus, the executive branch moved to keep open the lines of communication with the Assad government.*

On October 30, 1975, President Ford asked Congress for $90 million in assistance to support the security of Syria. "This assistance," declared Ford, "would enable our development cooperation with Syria to go forward, furthering our efforts to re-establish more normal bilateral relations."[80]

Responding favorably to the president's request, the legislative

---

*After a seven-year lapse the United States resumed diplomatic relations with Syria in June, 1974.

branch earmarked $90 million for Syria in the FY 1976 Foreign Assistance Appropriations Bill. In each of the three succeeding fiscal years (1977, 1978, and 1979), Syria was allocated $80 million, $90 million, and another $90 million, respectively. However, when Congress failed to pass a foreign assistance appropriations bill for fiscal 1980, Syria, under a continuing resolution, received only $15 million for the year ending September 30, 1980.

The House extended even that assistance grudgingly. While considering the FY 1979 Foreign Assistance Appropriations Bill (HR 12931), the House, by a 280–103 vote, approved an amendment by Edward Derwinski which cut the entire $90 million requested by President Carter for Syria. After the Senate restored that sum, House-Senate conferees approved retention of the $90 million, but also agreed to delete language that specified Syria as the beneficiary of those funds.

The following year (April 9, 1979), Derwinski again attempted to exclude any monies for Syria by attaching an amendment to that effect to the FY 1980 Foreign Assistance Authorization Bill (HR 3324). He maintained that if his 1978 amendment had prevailed, and "if this message . . . had reached the Syrian government, perhaps they would have adopted a more friendly attitude."

During floor debate, Representative Abner Mikva (D.-Ill.) professed his concern that Derwinski's amendment would not let "even a little window open in Syria. . . . I would at least rather [have Syria] have some dialog with the West rather than have them take all of their messages from the Soviet Union."

Congressman Hamilton sought to soften Derwinski's cut-off proposal by adding to it a phrase which would permit the president to grant aid if he "determines and reports to the Congress that assistance for Syria is in the national interests of the United States."[81] The Hamilton substitute was adopted 193–177, but the Derwinski-Hamilton Amendment was eventually stricken in conference. However, in another 1979 measure, the Foreign Military Authorization Act (HR 3173), Congress conditioned Syria's eligibility for economic support funds (formerly called security supporting assistance) upon presidential determination that the Assad regime was "acting in good faith to achieve further progress toward a comprehensive peace settlement in the Middle East."

Derwinski's next strike proved to be fatal. After losing in the Foreign Affairs Committee, the Illinois Republican moved on June 5,

1980, on the House floor to delete the $3.5 million in economic support funds allocated to Syria in the FY 1981 Foreign Aid Authorization Bill (HR 6942). In a May 22 "Dear Colleague" letter, Derwinski explained that "the current international climate dictates that the United States act like a great power and manifest its strength and resolve. . . . One way to begin redressing [our] sorry image is to stop begging people, who have consistently undermined our foreign policy objectives, to take our money—like Syria. . . . In short, we have spent five unproductive years in trying to cultivate the Syrian government. It's time, therefore, to suspend our aid at least for a year and watch for positive developments."[82]

The Carter administration was anxious that the House reject Derwinski's move. The $3.5 million was to be spent to bring approximately one hundred Syrians to the United States to train them to become professionals in agriculture, rural development, education, human resources, and nutrition. In a memorandum to House members the State Department insisted that "the utility of this program cannot be overestimated. It is the one program we have with Syria which provides the U.S. with a means to establish lasting ties with present and future Syrian leaders.

"Our desire to continue despite [policy] difficulties is premised on long-term U.S. interests which require that we have the ability to work with Syria to achieve significant U.S. regional objectives and on our belief that having a cadre of U.S.-trained Syrian leaders will help us significantly in this process."[83]

This rationale was advanced by Representative Hamilton in rebuttal to Derwinski's arguments, but to no avail. The amendment carried, 329–71. During its consideration of HR 6942, although not citing Syria by name, the Senate reduced by $3.5 million the total level of economic support funds. The House language was ultimately reinstated by conferees, thus effectively denying any new aid for Syria in fiscal 1981.

After passage of his amendment, the "positive developments" awaited by Derwinski were soon forthcoming. On August 22, 1980, Syria's ruling Baath party, after a four-day meeting of its central committee, called for a strengthening of its country's links with Moscow. The central committee authorized the Assad government to begin a "quantitative development" in its relations with the Kremlin.[84]

Eleven days later, President Assad responded favorably to a call by President Qaddafi of Libya for a constitutional merger of their two nations. In his telegram to Qaddafi, Assad reportedly stated: "This unity appeal has struck an immediate favorable response among us. . . . We stand together on the past of unity. . . . We stretch out our hand to shake yours in order to begin at once the work to bring about this great goal."[85]

Consequently, by the fall of 1980 the two occurrences that the State Department had long struggled to prevent had materialized. Perhaps solidification of Soviet-Syrian relations and a Libyan-Syrian consolidation would have happened in the normal course of events. But House stridency did little to deter such steps.*

Human Rights—A House Initiative

In practically every instance House ventures in international affairs have been detours, usually temporary, on foreign-policy routes laid out by successive administrations. The notable exception has been human rights, a new road paved by the House in the early 1970s. Donald Fraser (D.-Minn.) and Tom Harkin (D.-Iowa) were the two men most closely identified with that initiative.

Subcommittee reforms advanced Fraser to the chairmanship of the Foreign Affairs Committee's Subcommittee on International Organizations in 1973. During Fraser's six-year chairmanship* this subcommittee held more than 150 hearings on human-rights problems which existed in over forty countries. In 1974 the International Organizations in 1973. During Fraser's six-year chairmanship[†] this subcommittee held more than 150 hearings on human-rights problems ing foreign policy. That recommendation was transcribed into law (PL 93-559) when the House, and later the Senate, incorporated into the Foreign Assistance Act of 1974 a provision urging (but not requiring) the president to reduce or terminate security assistance to any state that engages in a consistent pattern of gross violations of internationally recognized human rights. Transgressions specifically defined by PL 93-559 are torture; cruel, inhuman, or degrading treatment or punishment; prolonged detention without charges;

---

* By the end of 1981 prospects for a Libya-Syria merger had virtually vanished.

† In 1978, Fraser gave up his House seat to run for the Senate. He was defeated in the Democratic primary but in 1979 was elected mayor of Minneapolis.

other flagrant denials of the rights to life, liberty, and the security of persons.

After adopting that principle, Congress added a full range of human-rights provisions to its foreign-assistance programs. The Trade Act of 1974 (HR 10710) prohibited most-favored-nation (MFN) treatment for those "nonmarket" economies that restricted emigration. Although general in its applicability, that clause was aimed at the Soviet Union, which, over the years, had severely limited the exodus of its Jewish citizens.

The House also has singled out individual countries for aid denial. At one time or another Angola, Argentina, Brazil, Cambodia, the Central African Empire, Chile, Cuba, Laos, Mozambique, the Philippines, Syria, Tanzania, Uganda, and Vietnam have been on the House's "hit list."

But the framework for America's human-rights policies is found in the amendment introduced by Congressman Harkin on September 10, 1975. Attached to the 1975 Foreign Economic Aid Bill (HR 9005), Harkin's proposal barred any United States assistance to nations engaged in a consistent pattern of gross human-rights violations. This injunction could be waived if the president demonstrated to the Congress that the aid would directly benefit the needy people of the subject country and if neither the House nor the Senate disapproved within thirty days after submission of the president's report.

Representative Jonathan Bingham immediately saw the dangers of the Harkin plan. "What really troubles me . . . is that the President, every time any assistance is offered . . . would have a terrible responsibility. . . . He is going to have to decide whether a country is one which engages in a consistent pattern of gross violation of internationally recognized human rights. . . . Every time he files a statement, it would be, in effect, an insult to the country concerned, and would upset our relations with that country."[86]

Unimpressed by Bingham's doubts, the House approved the Harkin Amendment 238–164. James Abourezk (D.-S.D.) offered Harkin's amendment during Senate debate, and it was accepted without objection. Later, similar amendments, modeled on Harkin's economic assistance proscriptions, were appended to bills authorizing military aid and United States contributions to multilateral financial institutions.

Thus, Congress established the president and itself as the moral arbiters of the domestic behavior of nations. Each year, in accordance with section 116 (d) and 502 (b) of the Foreign Assistance Act, the Department of State must submit to the legislative branch a volume (854 pages in 1979) entitled *Country Reports on Human Rights Practices*. The 1979 report "graded" human-rights conditions in 154 nations. One country omitted from the report was the United States—if we were subject to the same judgment by other nations, it would be interesting to observe American reactions to a less-than-perfect rating!

Despite the perils described by Representative Bingham, Jimmy Carter, said Arthur Schlesinger, Jr., "seized the standard of human rights and succeeded in presenting it to the world as if it had been American property all along."[87] So, a new global objective—this one instigated by the legislative branch—was added to the list of America's international goals outlined earlier.

Abraham Lowenthal, director of the Latin American Studies Program of the Woodrow Wilson International Center for Scholars, ascribed to President Carter four motives for embarking upon his human-rights crusade: to restore American confidence and pride in its government; to regain the ideological offensive against Communist countries; to provide United States diplomats with a legitimate basis for communicating with opposition leaders in authoritarian settings; and to help protect thousands of actual and potential victims of human-rights violations.[88]

But as the Congress and the Carter Administration discovered, instituting human-rights policies is much like effecting tax reform— what is sound in theory becomes thorny in practice. One major problem involves conflicting objectives. For example, cooperation with a repressive government may be viewed as critical to our regional security aims. Therefore, in the Philippines, South Korea, Iran (under the shah), Greece (during the reign of the colonels), and Portugal (while it still maintained its African possessions), our pursuit of human rights was less vigorous than it was in those countries in which we had no special interest. For many foreign leaders the uneven application of the policy tends to create a cynical view of the United States commitment to human rights.

Raising the human-rights issue could also be counterproductive for those whom we seek to benefit. After Congress attached conditions to the extension of nondiscriminatory trade terms to Communist ("nonmarket") nations in 1974, Russia reduced its emigration quotas from 33,500 (in 1973) to 13,300 (in 1975).[89] In a very moving meeting in Moscow on April 2, 1975, Congressman Bingham and I were told by twenty Soviet Jews that although they were upset about the slowdown in emigration, they hoped that Congress, as a matter of principle, would continue to deny most-favored-nation status to Russia.*

Finally, the target country, on occasion, is able to retaliate against the United States. On January 14, 1975, Secretary Kissinger announced that the Soviets had rejected Congress's demands for emigration reform as a condition for nondiscriminatory trade terms and, accordingly, had canceled a 1972 commercial agreement with the United States which had helped open the way to détente. Russia later reneged on its World War II Lend-Lease repayments.

In 1977, disgruntled by the State Department's annual *Country Reports on Human Rights Practices*, Brazil renounced its long-standing military-assistance pact with the United States and rebuffed our $55-million sales credit offer. Later that year Brazil's president, Ernesto Giesel, was the only hemisphere leader who was absent from ceremonies for the signing of the Panama Canal treaties in Washington.

In 1977, accusing the United States of meddling in its internal affairs, Argentina refused all American aid linked to human rights. In January 1980, Argentina declined to join our government's boycott on grain sales to the Soviet Union. The Foreign Ministry stated that "we refuse to take part in punitive decisions . . . which were adopted without our prior participation or which are taken in centers of decision outside our country."[90] The real reason for its action, State Department officials opined, was Argentina's disaffection with our human-rights criticisms.

The fundamental question, of course, is Have congressional-presidential actions succeeded in improving human rights practices throughout the world? Writing in *International Studies Quarterly*, former representative Fraser pointed out that "we cannot take credit for human-rights advances, because to do so tends to be destructive."[91] But, as *International Herald Tribune* correspondent Jonathan Power reported, "It's a more democratic and less repressive

---

*The quota was raised to 51,400 in 1979. Many observers believed the Soviets took this action to produce a more favorable climate during the Senate's SALT II debate.

world than it was." It is difficult to attribute this to American policy, Power noted, "since cause and effect often appear so far apart."[92]

Yet Abraham Lowenthal discovered specific results from United States human-rights efforts. "Thousands of Latin Americans have been helped directly, and scores of others pre-emptively, because of the Carter policies. Significant numbers of political prisoners have been released in Chile, Cuba, Paraguay, and Haiti, and some have been let go in several other countries. In almost every case, U.S. pressure appears to have helped secure their release."

Lowenthal also indicated that the use of torture decreased throughout the region, and numerous Latin Americans whom he interviewed advised him that American persuasion prevented many atrocities in their countries, especially by the local military establishments.[93]

In the light of these apparent successes, it is predictable that the House's interest in human rights will continue. This certainly was the view of Charles Vanik (D.-Ohio), author of the emigration restrictions in the 1974 Trade Act. Vanik, who retired at the end of the Ninety-Sixth Congress, expressed the opinion that human-rights activity by House members would accelerate in the future.[94] It is a "no-lose" proposition. The cause is right, and House members, to the applause of their constituents, can posture about their human-rights positions without fear of electoral retribution from abroad.

Conclusion

Sipping his coffee one morning in the House dining room, Speaker "Tip" O'Neill ruminated about the House's new outspokenness on sensitive international questions. "We used to have a bipartisan foreign policy. If a member didn't like a particular proposal, he would swallow hard and support the president. Today we no longer have a bipartisan foreign policy. Everyone is for himself even though he knows little about international issues. Some professor comes up with an idea, gives it to a congressman, who, in turn, introduces it as an amendment."[95]

Ironically, it was O'Neill himself who opened the door to these amendments. His proposed rules revision, adopted by the House in 1970, made it possible to obtain recorded votes on floor amendments. This procedural change served as a magnet for every conceivable foreign-policy interest. The result was an almost fourfold (from 44 to 155) increase between 1969 and 1979 in the number of foreign-policy amendments introduced by House members (Tables 2 and 3).

Among the earliest were those offered by representatives seeking to end our military involvement in Southeast Asia. Fourteen attempts ended in failure. Success, as we have already observed, came only after public opinion had forced removal of all of our forces from Indochina. While a case can be made that the earlier floor debates created the climate for this troop withdrawal, one also can conclude that the House followed, rather than shaped, citizen attitudes.

With the possible exception of human rights, floor amendments have not attempted to redirect our international goals. They have merely sought to impose limitations on a foreign-policy agenda already established and submitted to Congress by the executive branch. Moreover, by 1980 the House had begun to retreat from its earlier reforms aimed at giving it more oversight of executive initiatives. It eased requirements for reporting by the CIA, was less than forceful in pursuing the authority granted it under the War Powers Resolution, and liberalized foreign military sales restrictions. Confronted with the difficult choices posed by the new procedures for arriving at the budget, the House in 1979, 1980, and 1981 allowed that process to deteriorate to such an extent that important international programs were shortchanged to the detriment of our own economy.

The environment in which House members consider floor amendments is hardly conducive to rational decision making. As previously described, little time is spent in considering amendments. Few members are in attendance during floor debate. Votes are cast without benefit of facts or awareness of possible results. The decentralization of an already fragmented body, as noted in chapter 4, has made it extremely difficult for House leaders and administration officials to forestall acceptance of potentially damaging foreign-policy amendments.

"The results," said MIT professor William E. Griffith (a roving editor for *Reader's Digest*), "in nearly every case, have been self-defeating and contrary to our national interest."[96] Griffith's discouraging assessment is well supported by fact. First, in each instance the House's foreign-policy actions described in the preceding pages were opposed by the executive branch. Second, in no case did these efforts commence in House committees with foreign-policy expertise and jurisdiction. Rather, they were initiated (or ratified, if originated by the Senate) on the House floor. Third, nationwide editorial opposition was directed toward seven of the amendments. Fourth, in response to House moves, censure resolutions were adopted by seven international bodies: the United Nations Security Council, the United Nations General Assembly, the United Nations Administration Committee on Coordination, the Permanent Council of the Organization of American States, the General Assembly of the Organization of American States, the Organization of African Unity, and the International Bank for Reconstruction and Development. Fifth, with one exception (Congressman Derwinski's Syrian amendment), every "self-defeating" step taken by the House was later reversed.

Out-of-town newspapers and international organs, of course, have little or no force in a representative's district. Constituents do. It is understandable, therefore, that members are more concerned about the reaction of the "folks back home" than they are about criticism from media located in other cities or condemnations by international forums. It is this instinct for survival, rather than regard for our global aims, that dominates the voting considerations of many House members.

CHAPTER 6

Getting Elected to the New House

The question of what motivates a member of the House of Representatives has long intrigued students of the legislative branch. Richard Fenno found that the most widely held goals among congressmen are reelection, influence within the House, and good public policy.[1] In his book *Congress: The Electoral Connection*, David Mayhew cited reelection as the principal focus of House members' activities. To that end, Mayhew maintained, much of the legislators' energies are expended in self-advertising, claiming credit, and taking positions (Mayhew noted that making a stand on an issue is often more important to the member than winning it).[2]

Lawrence Dodd, co-editor of *Congress Reconsidered*, concluded that "virtually all members of the U.S. Congress are preoccupied with power considerations" (a notion also stressed by Rochelle Jones and Peter Woll in their 1979 book *The Private World of Congress*). Dodd recognized, however, that "re-election is necessary in order to remain in the struggle within Congress for power position."[3] Clearly, while motivation differs with individual House members, all share one common objective—reelection!

The Value of Incumbency

In the eleven congressional elections held during the period 1960–80, House members were remarkably adept at retaining their seats. As Table 4 reveals, their "success rate," which reached a high of 96.8 percent in 1968, fell below 90 percent only three times. Even in 1964 and 1974—the years of the Johnson landslide and the Watergate debacle—incumbents won 87 percent of the House races. The so-called marginal* seats are also disappearing. In 1960, of the 400 House incumbents running in the general election, 58.9 percent secured at least 60 percent of the vote. In 1980, 278 of the 392 members seeking reelection (71 percent) won by margins of 60 percent or more. An insightful explanation of the growing difficulty of unseating incumbents appeared in Morris Fiorina's 1977 publication *Congress: Keystone of the Washington Establishment:* "The growth of an activist federal government has stimulated a change in the mix of congressional activities. Specifically, a lesser proportion of congressional effort is now going into programmatic activities and a greater proportion of pork-barrel and casework activities. As a result, today's congressmen make relatively fewer enemies and relatively more friends among the people of their district."[4]

Fiorina's findings compared with my own door-to-door campaign experiences (I walked approximately five hundred miles in each of my five reelection efforts). It was a rare precinct in which I did not receive several "thank-you's" ("I've been meaning to write you") for my assistance in allaying constituent problems. Such cues simplified the task of developing a campaign theme—in each reelection quest my advertising agency saturated the airwaves with a catchy jingle imploring voters to "keep Whalen working for you."

But casework and grant announcements are not the only weapons in the incumbent's reelection arsenal. House Post Office figures indicate that in 1979, on the average, each member sent four hundred thousand pieces of mail.[5] Included in this melange were district-wide newsletters, constituent questionnaires, and computerized special-interest missives. A representative's computer data bank (either operated in-house or by Washington-area firms) might contain a profile of each constituent; dates of any communications received; views regarding each issue discussed in those letters; dates and nature of the member's response; appropriate salutation ("Dear Jack," not "John"); party affiliation; residence by ward and precinct.

---

* Marginal seats are held by those incumbents who received less than 60 percent of the major party vote in the last election. The 1960 figures were obtained from Albert Cover and David Mayhew's article "Congressional Dynamics and the Decline of Competitive Congressional Elections" in *Congress Reconsidered* (New York: Praeger, 1976), p. 55; the 1980 percentage was extracted from the November 8, 1980, issue of *Congressional Quarterly Weekly Report*, pp. 3338–45.

Radio and television studios are available to the congressman who wishes to send tapes to local stations. With the advent of continuous television coverage of floor proceedings, House members can now beam their messages directly to viewers in their districts. By the end of 1980 the House broadcast signal was being transmitted by the Cable-Satellite Public Affairs Network (C-SPAN) to one thousand of the nation's four thousand cable television systems representing a potential viewing audience of 3.5 million homes. Floor action is also picked up by public-affairs shows as well as by the three commercial television networks, which frequently use excerpts of debates in their evening news programs.

The effect of these possibilities for exposure has dramatically affected floor proceedings. The number of one-minute speeches* delivered by members has shown a marked increase since television broadcasts began on February 19, 1979 (for instance, 110 in March 1977; 268 in March 1980). In December 1979 the Committee on House Administration sent a questionnaire to all members requesting their views concerning the operation of the broadcast system. Of the 297 who replied, 68 percent said the television cameras in the chamber had no influence on their floor attendance, and 88 percent indicated that they made no speeches that would not have been given were it not for the presence of the cameras. However, 77 percent believed their colleagues were giving more speeches because of the televised proceedings, and 48 percent expressed the opinion that television was a factor in the rise in the number of floor amendments being offered.[6]

Additional advantages for the incumbent include the periodic columns that the local newspapers are pleased to feature. Office-expense accounts now permit unlimited travel to the district (in 1967 only four trips per year were reimbursable). While at home, the member enjoys celebrity status; is the subject of frequent media interviews; sits at the head table (even if he is not the featured speaker) at civic, social and political gatherings; makes flag presentations to veterans organizations, school groups, Boy Scout and Girl Scout troops; throws out the first ball at athletic contests; occupies the lead car in holiday parades; consumes inordinate amounts of

---

*Following the chaplain's opening prayer, the speaker usually grants unanimous consent requests by members to address the House for one minute on topics of their own choosing.

goulash, bratwurst, and spaghetti at ethnic picnics; and draws the winning raffle ticket at parish festivals.

Until 1971 House members could avoid most politically embarrassing policy questions while back in their districts. Operating behind the protective shroud of committee secrecy and unrecorded votes on floor amendments, representatives were not besieged by indignant constituents inquiring why they voted as they did on a particular issue. Now, thanks to the procedural reforms of the 1970s, the policy preferences of House members have become more visible. A scorecard is kept on every conceivable issue. No longer, therefore, can a member obfuscate his or her position on such questions as the funding of United Nations programs, indirect and direct aid to socialist and communist states, economic and military assistance to Arab nations, transfer of Canal Zone sovereignty to the government of Panama, human rights, trade preferences to Latin American OPEC members, Rhodesian sanctions, and arms sales to Turkey.

Public Interest in Foreign Policy

According to the conventional wisdom, the public is not really interested in international affairs, so presumably House members have little to fear in the greater accessibility of their voting records on specific foreign-policy issues. Polling data affirm the first part of this assumption. For instance, when asked by the Gallup organization, "What do you think will be the most important national issues in the coming 1974 congressional elections?" 2,384 Republican county chairmen made the following assessment:

	Percent
High cost of living/inflation	71
Energy crisis/fuel shortages	65
Watergate/honesty in government	32
International problems: maintaining peace, dealing with Russia, Mideast situation, national defense, foreign aid	10

	Percent
Unemployment	7
Campaign financing, election reform	3
Environment/ecology/land use	2
	190

(Totals add to more than 100 percent because of multiple responses.)[7]

In an October 12, 1978, poll "international problems, foreign policy" received only a 6-percent rating (out of a 116 percent total) from Gallup respondees.[8]

The reason for this low interest, suggested political scientist Lester Milbrath, is that most foreign-policy issues have no direct and identifiable impact on any segment of the population.[9] Barry Hughes emphasized this point in *The Domestic Context of American Foreign Policy*: "it is useful to make a distinction between (1) a very few salient foreign policy issues (such as Korea and Vietnam), about which the public does become concerned and (2) the vast majority of foreign policy activities, about which most of the public is either unaware or uninformed."[10]

Thus, as Aage Clausen concluded in *How Congressmen Decide: A Policy Focus*, it is only a "limited number of constituents who maintain a steady interest in foreign affairs and form a specialized public on foreign policy questions." Among these "elites," Clausen included newspaper editors as well as labor, business, farm, professional, and political leaders.[11]

What foreign-policy communications representatives do receive usually come from three sources: ethnic or religious lobbies; economic associations; and ideological affinity organizations. Contact from members of these groups is infrequent and usually limited to a specialized subject. Jewish agencies, for example, concentrate on Middle East issues—aid to Israel and arms sales to Arab nations. Greek-Americans bombarded the House in 1974–75 with letters opposing the transfer of military equipment to Turkey. "Doc" Morgan, chairman of the Foreign Affairs Committee, testified, "I have been around for 30 years and I have never in my life been pressured by any company or union like I was by the particular ethnic group interested in that [arm sales to Turkey] issue."[12] The AFL-CIO, the

United States Chamber of Commerce, and the National Association of Manufacturers (NAM) are most active in trade matters (witness the AFL-CIO's attempt in 1973 to secure import quotas and limitations on investment abroad). Ideological organizations of both the right and the left have spoken out on Vietnam, military spending levels, arms control, global hunger, and other Third World problems.

When pressure is exerted by these groups, there exists no effective countervailing force to which the House member may turn for support. "There has been a terrible job done in developing a constituency for United States' non-military foreign commitments," observed Representative Timothy Wirth (D.-Colo.).[13] Congressmen, therefore, gain few points by bucking a strong foreign-policy lobbying assault.

These exceptional cases aside, constituent interest in foreign policy is small, but this does not free the House Member to vote as he or she chooses without concern for possible electoral damage. That "well-informed constituent opinion does not exist"[14] is, in fact, fast becoming a danger, not a blessing, to the average congressman, for ignorance of the facts can often lead voters to serious misperceptions of representatives' foreign-policy views. To understand that statement one must be aware of the atmosphere in which recent congressional elections have been held and the strategies employed within that climate by the candidates and their committees.

The Electoral Process

Preceding each campaign, the incumbent has an eighteen-month nonconfrontational period during which to exercise the previously described "self-advertising" perquisites. When the race officially begins, candidates face an electorate with a short attention span. Messages, therefore, must be compressed in a twenty-to-sixty-second commercial on radio or television or in a hand-out or newspaper advertisement that can be scanned and discarded in less than a minute. This leaves no time for a refined and intelligible presentation of issues. Instead, the contest becomes one of *image*. Instead of dwelling on specific legislative positions, incumbent House members must "point with pride," stressing experience, constituent service, committee ranking, and grants obtained for the district * (hence the slogan "Keep Whalen Working for You").

The nonincumbent, to gain public attention, must create an *image difference*, which usually casts the House member in a negative light. This often involves taking out of context several of the incumbent's votes, usually on floor amendments, and portraying them in a way that attracts the critical attention of individuals and organizations devoted to one or another cause.

Let a politically astute central states Republican congressman describe this process.

> "Single issue" groups go way back in our history . . . the Abolitionists, for instance. A new group of single issue organizations has emerged: (1) gun control opponents; (2) antiabortionists; (3) fundamental religionists. To these three I would add the ardent nationalists and anticommunists. One "single issue" group, by itself, does not win an election. "Prolife" advocates, for example, were not sufficient to defeat Senator Dick Clark (D.-Iowa) in 1978—it's the "double" or "triple" interest groups, in concert, often trading lists, who swing the election. What they have done is to create, for the first time, an *image* of the Congressman as a "liberal." Heretofore, this is something that the incumbent was able to avoid.
>
> In 1977, 26 percent of those responding to an Iowa poll labelled Senator Clark a conservative. On Election Day, due to the constant drumming by several issue groups, only one percent, in a similar poll, believed Clark to be a conservative. These negative approaches are perhaps unfortunate, for often they result in both parties selecting candidates from among the extremes of their respective camps. Thus, the "middle" becomes underrepresented in the general election.

Establishing a "Difference"

Like single-interest groups, the politics of coalescence is not new to the American scene. After the Depression thrust him into the presidency, Franklin Roosevelt, building upon his party's traditional

---

* Most federal grants to local governments and agencies are automatic. However, when he served as President Kennedy's chief congressional operative, Lawrence

southern base, attracted organized labor, blacks, farmers, and the middle class to the Democratic ranks. In the late 1960s and early 1970s an agglomeration of civil-rights advocates, antiwar militants, and environmentalists (remember their attack on Congress's "Dirty Dozen"?) helped alter the makeup of the House of Representatives. In the modern electoral climate, where issues and messages must be packaged to fit the formats of television and high-impact advertising, the politics of getting along with cause-oriented coalitions have changed.

In the 1978 general election, Thomas Foley, a Washington Democrat, became a target of the negative image makers. Among the most popular and effective members of the House, Foley was chairman of both the Democratic Caucus and the Agriculture Committee. But sensing that Foley was vulnerable, a number of his constituents formed the Fifth District Congressional Club for the sole purpose of bringing him down. How they proposed to do this was related in the April 28, 1978, edition of the Spokane *Argus* by reporter William Stimson. The techniques cited in Stimson's story are typical of those employed in many other congressional races throughout the country.

> The group has gone to Washington, D.C., to hire a professional political campaign advisor and to Southern California for a professional pollster. Unfortunately, the store-boughten strategy seems to boil down to: figure out what voters are against and then distort Foley's record as much as required to show he's for it.
>
> The hired political advisor combed Foley's voting record for evidence of differences with the constituents back home. The pollster, meanwhile, sampled opinion in the Fifth District to find out if it was at variance with Foley's votes.
>
> Sure enough, it was found that the people back home disagree with, among other things, Foley's insistence on giving foreign aid to Cuba and Cambodia. . . .
>
> Newspaper ads and mass mailing were arranged to advertise these views by Foley. At a press conference the diver-

O'Brien developed a system whereby the department making the award notified the congressman before releasing the funds. This gives the representative an opportunity to claim credit by making the grant announcement.

gence between Congressman and constituents was
announced.

The reference in the press conference to Foley's support of foreign aid to Cuba, Cambodia, and other Communist countries was,
of course, a distorted interpretation of his opposition to the Young
"no indirect aid" amendment, described in chapter 5. Foley, in fact,
neither favored nor voted for assistance to these countries. What he
did was to oppose a motion that, by violating the World Bank's charter, would have caused our expulsion from that organization. Instead, he voted for a compromise that instructed American delegates to the bank to vote against loans to the countries in question.

Stimson concluded his article by questioning the ethics of the
way in which Foley's voting record was depicted by the Fifth District Congressional Club. "Both the hired political campaign professional and the pollster say they see no intellectual dishonesty here.
They contend that if it's possible to make a plausible case that Foley
was voting as charged, it's up to him to *explain* [emphasis added]
any subtleties he thinks may be important. Whatever 'plausible
case' means, it doesn't have anything to do with the truth, and inso-
far as the campaign, it will be a sham." [15]

The Fifth District Congressional Club's theme was picked up by
Foley's general-election opponent, Duane Alton. Referring to for-
eign- as well as domestic-policy votes, Alton's literature accused
the Democratic incumbent of helping foreign producers compete
against eastern Washington farmers, supporting foreign aid to Communist nations, favoring "forced" school busing, harming social
security recipients, and boosting gun control. [16] On November 7,
1978, Foley squeaked to a narrow 8,440-vote victory (77,201 –
68,761). Foley again survived in 1980, defeating his Republican con-
testor by a 7,400-vote differential.

Republican House members are not immune from the "imagery"
game. For example, in 1980, Representative Paul Findley of Illinois's
Twentieth District, in a quotation appearing in a fund-raising advertisement sponsored by his opponent's committee, was tarred as
a "practicing anti-Semite who is one of the worst enemies that
Jews and Israel ever faced in the history of the U.S. Congress." [17] First
elected in 1960, Findley, who was the third-ranking Republican on
the Foreign Affairs Committee in 1980, actively supported aid for

Israel throughout his congressional career. The anti-Semitic charges made by Democrat David Robinson sprang from Findley's two visits with Yasser Arafat of the Palestine Liberation Organization (PLO) and his rebukes of Israel for that nation's settlement policies and bombardments of southern Lebanon.

In defending those actions, Findley stated, "I believe in Israel's right to exist. I have met with Prime Minister [Menachem] Begin twice and encouraged him to enter into joint agricultural projects with Egypt. I have also challenged him on the West Bank settlement policy and East Jerusalem." Findley advised syndicated columnist Nick Thimmesch that he saw Arafat because he felt the United States should maintain contact with all Third World pariahs, including Cuba, North Korea, Vietnam, South Yemen, and the Palestinians. Although a number of legislators, including Senator Charles Mathias, Senator Adlai Stevenson (D.-Ill.), and Senate Minority Leader Howard Baker (R.-Tenn.), visited Arafat once, "the difference," said Findley, "is that I met twice and encouraged others to meet him also."

David Brody, an official of the B'nai B'rith's Anti-Defamation League, said that he was "aghast with that [Robinson's] ad. However opposed we are to the PLO, it is sinful to characterize Findley as an anti-Semite. Jews disapprove of these tactics."[18] Notwithstanding the outpouring of contributions that the newspaper solicitation generated, Robinson's heavily financed campaign effort failed to depose Findley, who garnered 56 percent of the vote on November 4, 1980. But even in victory, one of Findley's staff assistants, reflecting a growing fear among Congress-watchers, told me, "You know, the problem is the good guys get tired of it. They don't have to take that crap, and just decide to drop out."

One Republican who was in this position in 1978 decided, to his later regret, not to drop out. In that year residents of Birmingham, Alabama, formed a Sixth District Committee for Better Representation in Congress to unseat John Buchanan in the September GOP primary. In a March 22, 1978, letter, Committee Chairman Sam N. Cole wrote to prospective donors that he was highly disturbed because Buchanan "personally sponsored legislation to finance the negotiation of the Panama Canal Treaties now being debated in the U.S. Senate; supports Carter's African policy with votes to boycott Rhodesia and to support its neighboring marxist regimes who sponsor guerilla attacks."[19]

In August, Buchanan's primary opponent, Albert Lee Smith, distributed the *Voting Scorecard for John Buchanan* showing how the incumbent voted on twelve "critical" issues. The flier claimed that Buchanan supported "$100 million to Communist Marxist African Dictatorships (HR 6884—5/24/77); Funding Panama Canal Treaty Giveaway (His Amendments to HR 6889—5/7/77); $7 Billion in Foreign Aid Giveaways (HR 7797—10/18/77)."[20]

Buchanan narrowly survived the 1978 primary, defeating Smith by only 2,410 votes (he rolled up a 61.7 percent majority in the November general election). But in a September 2, 1980, primary rematch, Buchanan was not as lucky, succumbing to Smith 25,531 to 20,691.

John Anderson (R.-Ill.), chairman of the Republican Conference, encountered many of the same charges in his 1978 primary race. His adversary's committee (Friends of Don Lyon) published a *John B. Anderson Voted* circular which listed the incumbent for "allowing negotiations to continue that would surrender the Panama Canal (H.R. 8121); $1.7 Billion for Foreign Aid (H.R. 6714); $3.2 Billion for *More* Foreign Aid (H.R. 6884)."[21]

Anderson's campaign staff prepared a twelve-page single-spaced response which elaborated the incumbent's views on the nineteen votes outlined in the Lyon committee's release. The problem, of course, was that it took too long to read and digest the Anderson rebuttal, much less understand the legislative nuances that it attempted to explain.

Like Buchanan, Anderson won his March 1978 primary and went on to win the November general election. But unlike Buchanan, the Illinois Republican became a "drop out," forsaking his House seat in 1980 for an unsuccessful run at the presidency.

In 1980, Christopher Dodd, who was serving his third term as representative from Connecticut's Second District, decided to seek the job being vacated by the Nutmeg State's senior senator, Abraham Ribicoff. His candidacy was in its infancy when the image-makers set out to establish the "Dodd difference." On February 1, 1980, a group of Connecticut citizens announced the formation of the You Can't Afford Chris Dodd Committee. At the same time they released *Chris Dodd's Record of Shame*, which showed that on "June 21, 1979: H.R. 111: Dodd votes to give away the Panama Canal; August 3, 1978: Dodd votes for aid to Idi Amin and communist Vietnam; August 14, 1978: H.R. 2931: Dodd votes for over $7 billion in foreign aid."

Like the circulars aimed at Foley, Buchanan, and Anderson, the *Record of Shame* coupled Dodd's foreign-policy votes with his "positions" on national defense, the economy, abortion, and gun control.[22] Despite their early start, Dodd's detractors failed to stop his bid for the Senate. On November 4, 1980, the Second District congressman outpolled Republican candidate (and former one-term New York senator) James Buckley by 190,000 votes.

By 1980, Arizona's ten-term Democratic Congressman,[*] Morris K. (Mo) Udall, had become a national celebrity. He had attracted country-wide attention in his run for the presidency in 1976 and earned great respect for his work as chairman of the House Interior and Insular Affairs Committee. But a legislator's fame and Washington honors often mean very little to constituents, a fact of which Mo Udall was well aware. A winner by only 9,181 votes in 1978, the Second District representative engaged in another hotly contested race two years later.

In 1980, Udall was confronted with a campaign based on an assortment of isolated, contextually unexplained floor votes designed to paint him as a captive of the "Far Left." During the summer a John Birch Society publication, *The Review of the News* (July 2, 1980, edition), mysteriously appeared on Tucson doorsteps. Attached was a note, "I thought you might be interested in this," signed by a "concerned neighbor." (Udall's opponent disclaimed any knowledge of this effort.) The article to which the "concerned neighbor" referred was one by Robert W. Lee which reviewed Udall's votes on "selected issues." In the international realm Lee accused Udall of an

> inclination to place roadblocks in the paths of America's friends while assisting her enemies. Regarding the former, for example, representative Udall has voted to: Denounce the Government of friendly, anti-Communist South Africa (October 31, 1977) . . . ; Repeal the Byrd Amendment which allowed importation of chrome ore from anti-Communist Rhodesia (March 4, 1977). Udall thus helped force the U.S. into compliance with the immoral, double-standard U.N. boycott of Rhodesia. . . .
>
> In contrast to this treatment of pro-Western Governments, consider Congressman Udall's votes to: Defeat an amendment

---

[*] Udall was sworn in as a member of Congress on May 2, 1961, after winning a special election to replace his brother, who had resigned to become secretary of the interior.

to prohibit the use of any funds in a State Department authorization bill for reparations or aid to the assassins in Communist Vietnam (May 4, 1977) . . . ; Kill an amendment to prohibit international financial institutions from using U.S. funds for aiding the brutal Communist regimes in Cuba, Laos, or Vietnam (April 6, 1977) . . . ; Thwart an amendment to prohibit foreign aid funds from being sent *indirectly* (through multilateral lending institutions to which we contribute, such as the World Bank), as well as directly, to the dictatorships of Uganda, Cambodia, Laos, or Vietnam (August 3, 1978); Scotch an amendment to prohibit any aid to Nicaragua without prior congressional approval, thus allowing the President unilaterally to aid the Communist regime which now controls that country (September 9, 1979).[23]

Despite the conservative trend that prevailed elsewhere in 1980, Udall not only won reelection but actually bettered his 1978 performance, accumulating 58 percent of the Second District vote.

Soft-spoken Joseph L. Fisher (D.-Va.), holder of a Harvard Ph.D. in economics (1947), was one of the House's most erudite members. His background made him a natural for the tax-writing Ways and Means Committee, to which he was appointed in his first term (1975), a rare assignment for a freshman. In 1977 he was selected by the leadership to serve on the powerful Budget Committee. Fisher's knowledge and objectivity made him a valuable resource to representatives seeking lucid explanations of the complex fiscal matters confronting the Congress.

But one vote on an obscure floor amendment helped bring an end to Fisher's distinguished legislative career. In 1980 his vote against the Ashbrook amendment to the FY 1981 Labor, Human Health and Human Services, Education Appropriations Bill (see chapter 5) became the dominant issue in Virginia's Tenth District congressional race. Fisher was accused by his Republican opponent, Frank R. Wolf, of supporting bilingual education, an unpopular proposition in the Tenth District, where scores of refugee families had settled. According to *Washington Post* staff writer Ed Bruske, Fairfax County officials feared that enforcement of bilingual education regulations would require teaching in as many as fifty different tongues in elementary schools, at a cost of many millions of dollars.

During campaign debates, Fisher denied that he ever voted for bilingual education, to which Wolf retorted, "Yes, you did, Joe. You may not think you did, but you did." The distinction between voting "against" a proposed legislative restriction and "for" a program toward which that prohibition is directed is a subtle one. While, technically, Fisher did not support the funding of bilingual education in voting against the Ashbrook amendment, this nuance was lost on his listeners and led to Wolf's charge of "double talk."

In a preelection interview with reporter Bruske, Congressman Fisher expressed concern about a system in which elections may be decided on the turn of one issue. "I've voted probably 50,000 times, publicly, on every kind of issue. Think of it. Sometimes, it worries me."[24] Fisher's fears were well placed, for on November 4, 1980, he lost to Frank Wolf by six thousand votes.

Washington Star columnist Edwin M. Yoder, Jr., wrote of North Carolina's Sixth District representative, Richardson Preyer: "Wherever judiciousness of mind and integrity of character were needed, the House leadership learned to turn to Rich Preyer. . . . The common note of his special assignments in Congress was clear. All of them acknowledged a judicious temperament, a well stocked and penetrating mind, and the gentle and considerate manner to which he was born and bred. . . . He is one of the most remarkable public men of his generation."[25] Yoder's view of Preyer is shared by those of us of both parties who served with the North Carolina Democrat.

Yet Preyer was unexpectedly defeated in 1980, when his opponent, Eugene Johnston, was able to pin a "big spender" label on the Sixth District congressman. Johnston used the *Congressional Spending Study* of the National Taxpayers Union (NTU) as the spear on which to impale Preyer. In 1980, NTU analyzed every House vote affecting federal spending and determined a "Congressional Spending Score" for each member by dividing the total votes cast opposing increased expenditures or for reduced spending by the total number of issues on which the representative was recorded. For most readers of NTU's literature, those ratings had to be accepted on faith, since individual votes were not reproduced, "because of the complexity of the calculation and the matter . . . involved." Few recipients of an NTU pamphlet took the time to write for the list of votes that the organization promised to make available on request.

The NTU study branded those who received a score of 23 percent or less as "Big Spenders." Preyer, with a 19-percent rating, fell into that category.[26] This rating was used extensively by Johnston and his campaign committee in speeches, advertisements, and letters to the editor, and was an important point in a press conference featuring a NTU official. Preyer told Bill Keller, a correspondent for the *Congressional Quarterly Weekly Report*, that he tried to reply to the accusation, "but the explanation is always a little more complicated. . . . In our society, where you have to say it in 60 seconds, it is hard to refute."[27] This, in large measure, accounted for Preyer's slim thirty-three-hundred-vote loss on November 4, 1980.

In Ohio's Ninth District 1980 congressional battle, the same charge also was hurled at Representative Thomas L. (Lud) Ashley, recognized by Washington observers as Congress's most knowledgeable authority on the subject of housing. In a campaign tabloid, *For the Record*, distributed by the Ed Weber Congressional Committee, the thirteen-term congressman was censured for "consistently [voting] for the liberal big spending programs that are the root cause of the economic mess we find ourselves in today." Selected as an example of Ashley's "big spending" proclivities was his vote against a motion to slice the FY 1980 Foreign Aid Appropriations Bill by a total of 4 percent ($180 million).[28] What was not explained in the Weber literature was that even before the House's September 6, 1979, approval of the 4 percent reduction, the fiscal 1980 spending level was $3.1 billion below that established for fiscal 1979. Failing to counter this and similar "big spender" criticisms and hurt by high unemployment in Toledo, Ashley lost his seat to Ed Weber on November 4, 1980, by more than twenty-eight thousand votes.

The "big spender" approach was less successful in Ohio's Third District, which I formerly represented. Despite being characterized by his Republican opponent, Albert Sealy, as the cause of inflation, my successor, Congressman Tony Hall, gained a second term by a 59-percent margin. During the campaign one of the twelve positions for which Hall was reproved in a Sealy newspaper advertisement was his vote "against a 10% across-the-board cut in foreign aid even though Egypt and Israel were exempt from the cut."[29] Again not mentioned was the $3.1 billion foreign aid cutback previously achieved by the House.

Although it ran Sealy's advertisement, the *Dayton Daily News* voiced its displeasure with its contents in a July 6, 1980, editorial:

> Negative advertising is becoming a specialty of those challenging incumbents. . . . The ads are reminiscent of the cynical "soft on Communism" ugliness of the 1950s. Don't vote for me; vote against him. Daytonians are being treated to the

unsavory spectacle of low blow ads aimed at Democratic Rep. Tony Hall by Republican challenger Albert Sealy. Mr. Sealy has many qualities to recommend him, but has done little to emphasize those. . . . It is a campaign that appeals not to voters' intelligence or knowledge but to their desire to kick someone.[30]

The preceding are just a few examples of how nonincumbents, in order to develop a "difference," deduced simplistic, often twisted assumptions from House members' votes on complex bills and amendments. Unfortunately, especially when it comes to foreign policy, the typical American seems unwilling or unable to take the time to study the issues. It is this fact which dictates current political strategy.

Blunting the "Differences"

Expecting next week's opponent to launch a passing offensive against his squad, the astute football coach will contrive a game plan to neutralize the enemy attack. Similarly, incumbent House members assiduously prepare for their next contests (a process which usually commences the day after the election). Having seen what can happen to such colleagues as Tom Foley, Paul Findley, John Buchanan, John Anderson, Richardson Preyer, Joe Fisher, and Lud Ashley, many representatives embark upon a program of "damage limitation" designed to blur possible "differences" that future rivals might seek to create. This approach, simply stated, is "don't give them anything to shoot at."

This is a two-step strategy. First, the incumbent must try to avoid taking positions that require lengthy clarification (for example, why a vote against tying the hands of the World Bank, thus forfeiting our membership in that institution, is not a vote for aid to Idi Amin or Fidel Castro). As one northern Democrat told me, "The best vote is the one you don't have to explain."

Here is how one border-state Democrat justified his vote for the Young (no "direct" or "indirect" aid) Amendment. "It would have been hard to explain why I voted against such a 'good amendment.' I also voted against the Panama Canal conference report because this is one issue my folks back home *do* understand. I could never explain why I voted for it."

So, as John Kingdon wrote in *Congressmen's Voting Decisions*, when members find themselves in a position where they are unable to devise an acceptable explanation, "if they do not feel intensely about the matter, they often vote so as to avoid the predicament." In other words, "Let Bob McNamara worry about the World Bank, and I'll worry about getting re-elected."

Second, congressmen evaluate each issue with an eye to the next election campaign. As Kingdon observed: "Congressmen simply anticipate possible campaign occurrences and take them into account as they vote. . . . Even though it doesn't affect the election outcome [Foley and the others did win, after all], Congressmen often simply try to *avoid* [emphasis added] such an embarrassing situation."[31]

One practitioner of this style—a midwestern Democrat—described it a little more colorfully:

> The basic instinct here is for survival. So on a foreign-policy vote, the first thing to do is look at what the district reaction would be. They have a short attention span. Therefore, I cannot hold them long enough to explain my vote. This is not pure politics as taught by the political scientists, but it is the way things work here at the House.
>
> After looking at the political implications, I also look at someone on the committee whose judgment I trust. I would never admit this, but a member cannot know the facts about every vote. So we have to look to others on occasion for guidance. On the Syria vote we look to the Jewish members and our Jewish community. I look to the Black Caucus on African votes because I have a large, well-to-do black constituency.

A middle-Atlantic-state Republican expressed strong support for the work of international financial institutions. "They provide for Third World stability. We can combat Communist influence through IFI assistance." Despite this sentiment, over the years he voted for the Young Amendment "more than I should have." While not conceding that it was politically difficult not to do so, the congressman did admit that "foreign aid is unpopular in my district as evidenced by Bob Teeter's* polls."

---

* Robert Teeter, who heads a Detroit opinion-research company, is one of the country's most respected pollsters. I used his services in my 1966 and 1968 campaigns—his election projections were amazingly accurate.

Two veteran Democrats exemplified those who follow Kingdon's principle of anticipating possible campaign issues. A border-state member commented: "I have voted against foreign aid every year for twenty years. It is unpopular in my district, which is very poor. Had I voted for it, it would have become a campaign issue." This statement comes from a member from Texas. "I received many letters opposing the Panama Canal Treaty. Had I voted for the Implementation conference report or against Hansen's 1975 amendment, it would have become a campaign issue in my district."

Indeed, "It's unpopular in my district" was the one consistent theme among the motivations of the House members whom I interviewed. Without being asked, 36 percent volunteered this as the reason for voting as they did on specific foreign-policy issues.

This attitude reflects what I call the "Nixon syndrome." On July 18, 1968, while addressing a House Republican Conference breakfast which I attended, presidential candidate Richard Nixon was asked by Peter Frelinghuysen (R.-N.J.), "Dick, how should we vote today on the foreign-aid bill?" Frelinghuysen, who was to co-manage the measure for the Foreign Affairs Committee that afternoon, received little encouragement from Nixon's three-word reply—"Vote your districts." Realizing that if elected president he would have to bear the consequences of a foreign-aid defeat, Nixon later recanted: "Look, we must have a foreign-aid bill, so if you can see your way clear, I hope you will vote for it."

It is this penchant for self-preservation which prompted former assistant secretary of state William D. Rogers' plaint that "Congress cannot resist the temptation to play low politics with high policy. With the fate of the entire House . . . in the hands of the voters every 730 days . . . the temptation to pander to prejudice and emotion is overwhelming." [32]

Coping with Electoral "Temptations"

But some House members do eschew the allure of subordinating international concerns to reelection interests. There are those who are guided by a strong sense of conviction. A border-state Democrat stated: "I have a number of thought-out foreign-policy principles. I am an internationalist, so I support free trade and foreign assistance. I support a strong defense. I do not believe these views are incompatible." A midwestern Democrat assented: "I have studied in Europe. I lived three years in the Caribbean and have taken graduate studies in foreign relations. I feel competent, therefore, to make an independent judgment."

Some take their educational responsibilities seriously. Said an eastern Democrat: "I will not fall into a trap by responding to Viguerie's* charges. I will defend my record on a positive basis. I will tell my constituents why I voted for the Panama Canal and why its passage is important to the country." One southern Democrat became a "born again" internationalist largely because of his new committee assignment.

> I used to take the demagogic approach by telling my constituents that I opposed the Panama Canal Treaties. However, by virtue of my committee position, I decided to support the Implementation Bill. I took a hard line with my constituents. "Look, the Senate passed the treaties. If we don't honor them, we'll lose the canal now, not in twenty years."
>
> I spent a great deal of time educating my district appearing on talk shows and discussing the issue in newsletters. This helped defuse the issue.
>
> I found that many of my colleagues, while agreeing with my analyses, felt compelled to look to their constituencies and voted against the Implementation Bill.

Certain members defer to the one interest group—the Jewish lobby—which does have a stake in passage of foreign-assistance appropriations. One east-coast Republican explained that "I have a 35-percent Jewish constituency. So I vote for the Foreign Aid Bill, since half of it involves money for Israel. This is a political vote based on the makeup of my constituency." A freshmen Republican, worried about another close election in 1980, declared: "I have to look to my district. Since foreign aid is unpopular, I voted against it in 1979. But I caught so much hell from my Jewish community that I switched my vote in 1980."

For a west-coast Democrat, an antiwar activist prior to his election to Congress, the "moment of truth" came after the 1973 Middle East War. "I was under tremendous pressure from Jewish lead-

---

* Richard Viguerie is a highly successful direct-mail executive, specializing in conservative causes. His firm is located in Falls Church, Virginia.

ers to vote for $2 billion in military aid to Israel. They were in my office when the bells rang for the vote. They walked me to the House floor, and as they left they said, 'We pray that you vote right.' But I couldn't go counter to my conscience, so I voted no. One southern conservative Democrat, seeing this vote, came up and shook my hand and stated how much he admired my courage in the face of probable defeat in 1974. But later I was able to explain my vote to Jewish audiences and won again in 1974."

A number of members defend their foreign-policy votes by reversing the anti-Communist argument—"I voted for it because I don't want to lose Nicaragua to Cuba [Syria to the Russians, and so forth]." For others, the "conventional wisdom" still pertains—"Foreign policy is not an issue in my district." This is especially true in metropolitan centers where the expense of mounting a media blitz is enormous. One big-city Democrat said: "I have polled my district sixteen years, and every year they put foreign aid lowest on the spending poll. Nevertheless, I have voted for it every year. It is not an issue in my district because it is difficult to pinpoint issues in _____. Therefore, I have never had a television or radio spot aimed against me." Other urban-area members made similar observations about the impracticability of waging issue-oriented radio and television campaigns against them.

Finally, some representatives are considered unbeatable. In such cases it is difficult to attract the money and manpower necessary to undertake a campaign that highlights the incumbent's "differences" from his constituents. Often found in one-party districts, these "untouchables" are free to pursue their views without undue fear of retaliation. However, one member who had such security expressed concerned about slippage—"If your percentage drops, they will be more willing to take you on in the next election." Another member, who represented an overwhelmingly Democratic district, admitted that the fear of a primary challenge kept him on the "right" side on all votes affecting Israel.

Conclusion

For House members, the potential for electoral damage has been heightened by the reforms of the 1970s. Their increased visibility and the multiplying number of recorded votes on which they must

be counted have compounded the possibilities for giving opponents issues and alienating constituents. In short, the more decisions one must make, the more enemies one is likely to create.

The "survival instinct," common to all representatives, has engendered a sort of "speak no evil, do no evil" paranoia among many
members. For them, as a former senior Foreign Affairs Committee
counsel put it, their foreign-policy views "extend no further than
the next election." But by espousing positions that require no explanation, by attempting to placate a public which does not take the
time to inform itself, House members, as seen in chapter 5, often
subvert our broader international interests.

CHAPTER 7

The New House in a New Decade

The effects of House reforms upon those who are directly occupied in the day-to-day lawmaking process—the executive branch (as initiator and "seller"), the House leadership (as manager), and the individual member (as the ultimate decision maker)—can be easily seen and evaluated. In the final analysis, however, it is not the players but the American people to whom we must look in assessing the effects of the House's "decade of reform."

If one subscribes, as I do, to the principle that "public policy is public business," then one must agree that the citizenry benefits from House rules that have brought foreign-policy decisions into the sunlight and, by so doing, have made members more accountable for their actions. The populace also gains from having a House membership that can command greater informational resources.

But for most Americans, House reforms have not come without penalty. Attaining coherent, rational foreign-policy formulation, already difficult in a body in which "power is nowhere concentrated,"[1] has been made even more arduous by the decentralization that the reforms engendered. Furthermore, democratization has weakened the capacity of House leaders to lead and administration representatives to exposit. "Despite yeoman efforts to improve the system," proclaimed Congressman Bill Frenzel, "conditions have actually become worse."[2] Perhaps the most surprising criticism came from Representative Lucien Nedzi, one of the Armed Service Committee's "Fearless Five." Reflecting on his impending retirement from Congress in 1980, Nedzi said, "Things were better under Rivers [the hawkish chairman of the late 1960s]. At least things got done."[3]

The House's new openness, in fact, has had a paradoxical effect. Intended as a procedural mechanism to help the House correct the executive branch's foreign-policy mistakes of the late 1960s, it has created a climate in which the majority of members, reacting to pollings of public opinion, find it inexpedient to administer the necessary palliatives. Further, this sensitivity to shifting public sentiment is diminishing enforcement of those reforms aimed at achieving parity in policymaking with the executive. In 1980 many of the provisions of the budget act were ignored. Procedures established to gain for the House a share in the exercise of war powers, control of arms sales, and oversight of CIA activities were being vitiated. This retreat from the assertion of its newly won powers, suggested a Foreign Affairs Committee counsel, manifested an attitude of "I don't want to know; therefore, I'm not responsible," which he felt was becoming prevalent among House members.

Openness has also induced the offering of capricious foreign-policy amendments, often for political gain. Although other members recognize them as ill-advised, such measures are difficult to oppose, for fear of retribution in the next campaign. This, reasoned former senator Fulbright, means that "the resurgent legislature of the late 1970s . . . has gone in the wrong direction, carping and meddling in the service of special interests but scarcely asserting itself through reflective deliberation on basic issues of national interest."[4]

The Adverse Effects of the Reforms upon the Public

In general, the House has turned its back on many of the long-held goals and objectives of American foreign policy. This new jingoism, which ignores our country's global responsibilities, makes an already insecure world, and our position in it, even less stable. This statement can be supported by any number of examples.

For instance, Congress's reneging on our commitments to international financial institutions has not only brought into question America's reliability and leadership in the world but has also been deleterious to a United States economy which has become increasingly dependent on Third World development for export markets and sources of scarce materials vital to our industries. Furthermore, if the House had been successful in placing conditions on our contributions to various world-development agencies, those organizations would undoubtedly not be operating today. They would have been unable to cope with the chaos created by allowing each country to dictate how and where its assessments should be spent.

To cite other examples, House-initiated action undermined, for a time, NATO's strength in the eastern Mediterranean, and House positions have alienated several Arab leaders whose support is critical to our attaining an overall Middle East settlement. House attempts to disrupt the Rhodesian peace process, if successful, might have contributed to a continuation of guerilla warfare in that country and opened the door to major-power intrusion in southern Africa. If the legislation to implement the Panama Canal Treaties had been torpedoed by the House, the continued functioning of that waterway would have been imperiled and the possibility of armed conflict with the Panamanian National Guard enlarged.

Finally, by voting to withhold from Venezuela and Ecuador the opportunity for trade preferences and by impeding relief assistance to Nicaragua, as well as by its votes on the canal treaties, the House contributed to growing anti-American resentment throughout the hemisphere. Another House-originated amendment not only slowed the flow of Soviet Jewish émigrés in the mid-1970s but also precipitated a reduction in trade relations with Russia and threatened to revive the Cold War.

Whatever the consequences of the reforms, there is little chance that the House will revert to secret committee sessions, unpublished committee votes, and nonrecorded votes on Floor amendments. That battle was fought and convincingly won by Common Cause and other citizen-interest lobbies, and those organizations are unlikely to be challenged by House members on the issue—after all, how can one "explain" a vote for keeping constituents in the dark? Consequently, the problem becomes one of preserving the benefits of House reform while easing the strains that they have imposed upon the making of foreign and domestic policy.

Suggested "Reform of the Reforms"

Structures of Power

Catherine Rudder, formerly assistant professor of political science at the University of Georgia, concluded that, in order for the House to function, to produce responsible legislation, "structures of power are needed." Rudder considered the new budgetary process, the reactivated Democratic Caucus, and the two adjuncts to the party leadership (the Rules Committee and the Steering and Policy Committee) to be "deliberate efforts in this direction."[6]

However, since 1977, when Rudder's comments were published, it has become evident that the "power" that those edifices were to provide never materialized. Many congressional budgetary procedures, as already noted, were not followed in 1980. At the same time the leadership was employing its committee appointment powers to please, not coerce. In the Ninety-sixth Congress the Democratic Caucus abandoned any semblance of a policy role. Only four program proposals, two of which were noncontroversial, were presented to the caucus during the period February 28, 1979– September 17, 1980. One of these, a resolution on wage-price controls offered by Representative Ted Weiss (D.-N.Y.), was finally tabled after the New York legislator failed in seven tries to muster a quorum. The other, Congressman Toby Moffett's motion to continue existing crude-oil price controls, won caucus approval by a 138–69 margin. However, when Moffett sought to insert that provision in the Department of Energy Authorization Bill on October 11, 1979, he was deserted by 120 Democrats whose votes, when added to 137 Republican nays, were sufficient to scuttle his amendment.[7]

Committee Reform

The 1977 report of the Special Subcommittee on Investigations of the House Foreign Affairs Committee recognized that "Congress must solve the problem of overlapping and disparate committee jurisdiction if it is to play a coherent and effective role in the conduct of American foreign policy." To accomplish this, the subcommittee recommended that the "foreign affairs committees of both Houses must be accorded primary and principal responsibility for foreign affairs in Congress."[8] The report, incidentally, did not make clear whether the House Foreign Affairs and Senate Foreign Relations committees also should assume the financial jurisdiction that is now lodged in the appropriations committees of the two chambers. However, that question is immaterial, for pleas for any restructuring of House committees have fallen upon deaf ears in recent years.

In 1974 the jurisdictional realignments proposed by the House's bipartisan select (Bolling) committee, mentioned in chapter 2, were rejected by the Democratic Caucus. Explaining why a majority of subcommittee chairmen voted against the Bolling Report, O'Neill stated the obvious: "The name of the game is power and the boys don't want to give it up."[9]

In July 1976, acting upon a recommendation of the task force on house accounts, the House set up another bipartisan body of eight members and seven private citizens to study House administrative services. That panel (the Commission on Administrative Review), headed by David Obey (D.-Wis.), submitted to the House a series of recommendations affecting committee organization, administrative procedures, and methods of arbitrating alleged discriminatory House employment practices. Fifteen months of commission work went for naught, however, when the House defeated (160–252) the rule for consideration of the Obey Report on October 12, 1977.

Another round of discussions on Committee reorganization began in 1979 when the House established a fifteen-member Select Committee on Committees, chaired by third-term representative Jerry Patterson (D.-Cal.). The select committee's major proposal, which would have created a new house committee on energy, was ignored by the House. When its mandate expired on April 30, 1980, the Patterson Committee, according to the *Washington Post*, found that "its attempt to achieve step-by-step change has been no more successful than the 1974 effort at comprehensive committee reorganization, and concluded there is no way to change the system without making too many important members fighting mad."[10]

Joint Committee on National Security

For many years there has been widespread support for a joint House-Senate committee to allow international and defense specialists in both bodies to integrate their work on foreign and military policies. The beginnings of this concept, James Robinson pointed out, can be traced as far back as 1950, when Harold Lasswell made such a recommendation in his book *National Security and Individual Freedom*.[11] Later supporters of the idea included Vice-President Nelson Rockefeller, Foreign Affairs Committee Chairman Clement Zablocki, and the Murphy Commission on the Organization of Government for the Conduct of Foreign Policy.

Despite this array of distinguished supporters, the Foreign Affairs Committee's Special Subcommittee on Investigations concluded:

> Such a committee would not, in and of itself, be effective in correcting Congress' weaknesses, improving attitudes in Congress and the executive branch, and ameliorating the current state of executive-legislative relations.
>
> A joint committee composed of the leadership of Congress and senior members of the several committees concerned generally with foreign policy would be both unwieldy in size and too demanding on those who would compose its membership. It also would be incapable of solving some of the major impediments to effective congressional participation in foreign policy.[12]

And to these limitations must be added the House's oft-demonstrated fear of any kind of jurisdictional shuffle.

Floor Maneuvers

Those charged with steering foreign-policy legislation through the House have invented a number of tactics to defuse potentially "crippling" amendments. One approach is to accept the modification and hope that it will be rejected by the Senate and then excised by conferees. By the time the conference report reaches the House floor, the issue addressed by the deleted amendment has often subsided in importance.

Another device, of more recent origin, is the "substitute amendment" technique. On June 5, 1980, Majority Leader Jim Wright (D.-Tex.) employed this maneuver to neutralize Congressman Bauman's amendment to the Foreign Aid Authorization Bill (HR 6942) which would have prohibited any aid to Nicaragua. Should Nicaragua receive any funds authorized by HR 6942, Wright's substitute directed the president to "report to the Congress every ninety days during fiscal year 1981 on the internal situation in Nicaragua, particularly on its observance of the human rights of its citizens and progress in the establishment of democratic political institutions including an orderly system of free elections." Reminding members that Indonesia, Nigeria, and Egypt, which once appeared to have been "swallowed up into the orbit of the Soviet Union," had returned "to a good and friendly relationship with the United States," Wright contended that "we can do the same with Nicaragua."[13] Wright's oratory carried the day; his substitute was adopted by a vote of 243–144. Once approved, a substitute amendment is not subject to further amendment.*

The problem with this tactic, of course, is that the influence of such leaders as the speaker and the majority leader cannot be employed against every unfriendly amendment. It must be reserved for those judged most critical. But when used by others the "substitute amendment" stratagem has had only mixed success. For instance, on July 18, 1979, during House debate on the Foreign Assistance Appropriations Bill (HR 4473), Representative Bill Young moved to prohibit the International Development Association (a World Bank subsidiary) from using the United States contribution to make loans to Vietnam. Congressman Matthew McHugh (D.-N.Y.) offered a substitute which stated that the ban on the IDA's use of American funds in Vietnam should not bar that organization from expending United States monies in Egypt and Sudan. McHugh's language so confused Young and the other members in attendance that they accepted his amendment on a standing vote, 25–20.

Debate on HR 4473 was suspended the next afternoon and resumed on September 5, the day that Congress returned from its summer recess. This gave Young nearly seven weeks to reflect upon the effect of McHugh's amendment. The Florida legislator finally recognized what the House parliamentarian and the Treasury Department had already told McHugh—the substitute amendment effectively erased the Young language from the bill. Young then attempted to reverse McHugh's victory of July 18 by introducing a new amendment (detailed in chapter 5) which prohibited all "direct" and "indirect" assistance to Vietnam and four other countries. Before the House acted on that proposal, McHugh offered still another substitute which provided that Young's prohibition on "indirect" assistance to specific countries should not deter international financial institutions from using our assessed funds to aid Israel, Egypt, and other nations not excluded by HR 4473. No longer

---

*In 1981 this tactic was employed by Reagan's House supporters to secure, without further amendment, approval of the First Budget Resolution, and the Budget Reconciliation and Tax Reduction bills.

fooled, Young and his followers repelled the substitute 153–244, after which the Floridian's amendment passed 281–117.

Better Consultation by the Executive Branch

"From a legislative viewpoint," concluded members of the Foreign Affairs Committee's Special Subcommittee on Investigations, "the crux of the problem between the executive branch and the Congress in foreign policy today is the inadequate state of consultation between the two branches." In its report the subcommittee recommended that the State Department's consultative procedures be reinforced, with the foreign-affairs committees of both houses continuing to serve as focal points for consultation.[14]

The difficulty of executing that solution was made clear by Marshall Wright, former assistant secretary of state for congressional relations, when he testified before the subcommittee on July 20, 1976.

> It is simply a physical impossibility for anyone seriously engaged in consulting on foreign policy problems to deal with 500 people. The physical arrangements, themselves, though the best in the world, would preclude any meaningful consultation with that number of people, or a quarter of that number of people.
>
> Now this suggests that the Congress, if it wishes on a continuing basis to participate seriously in the foreign policy process, . . . simply must create a small representative body to discharge this consultative responsibility.[15]

Just the opposite, of course, has occurred. Individual members acting by themselves or on behalf of small partisan groups, not the House leaders or chairmen of committees with responsibility for foreign affairs, have initiated and supported the troublesome foreign-policy actions. Recognizing this trend toward greater member involvement in international issues, Wright maintained that, unless the House did delegate power to a representative and small group to act on its behalf, "then talk of full participation on a continuing basis in the foreign policy process [would be] baying at the moon."[16]

State of the World Report and Foreign-Policy-Posture Hearings

C. William Maynes, former assistant secretary of state for international organization affairs (now editor of *Foreign Policy*), encouraged resumption of the State of the World report inaugurated by President Nixon and Secretary Kissinger. Maynes suggested that such a document could serve as the starting point for annual hearings on our foreign-policy posture during which the administration could outline for Congress its current, intermediate, and long-range plans, to which members could then respond. By following this approach, Maynes continued, the executive branch would give Congress a broader perspective on international affairs and a greater sense of participation.[17]

Unfortunately, the same time demands that prevented most members from reading Kissinger's lengthy (but informative) commentaries would undoubtedly do so again if the State Department were to reinstate the report. Furthermore, since those earlier attempts had scant effect on the House's appetite for injudicious intrusion into the making of foreign-policy, the State Department, understandably, has little interest in renewing the reports. As for posture hearings, they would merely add another layer of testimony to the already overburdened schedules of the executive and legislative branches.

Upgrade the State Department's Office of Congressional Relations

Diplomat-scholar Robert G. Neumann proposed in 1977 that the rank presently accorded the head of the State Department's Office of Congressional Relations be raised to that of undersecretary of state. By carrying such a title, the undersecretary's "coordinating functions and his central position in advising the Secretary of State would be enhanced. His new rank would be telling evidence of the importance which the State Department attributes to congressional relations."[18] Neumann's call was echoed by the Special Subcommittee on Investigations, which concluded that "upgrading the office [from assistant to undersecretary] can give its holder more leverage in presenting congressional views, moods, intents, and demands in high-level discussions within the State Department."[19]

It is difficult to fathom how a mere change in nomenclature would bring more cordial and orderly relations between the House and the State Department. It would not alter the cast of characters; it would in no way diminish the number and complexity of two-way consultations; and it would not lessen the political pressures that confront House members when they vote on foreign-policy bills and amendments.

Developing a Foreign-Policy Constituency

Ambassador Neumann also believed that a constituency had to be developed to strengthen the State Department's lobbying capability. He recommended that the Office of Congressional Relations ascertain how our relations abroad affected the economic interests of business and labor, in what states those interests were located, and how they related to senators and representatives from that state. Neumann proposed that the State Department then "let a congressman know in advance when ongoing diplomatic relations are likely to affect business or labor interests in his constituency. These are the kinds of relationships which legislators understand well and take very much into consideration."[20]

As a former president (1978–80) of a public-interest lobby, New Directions, I know the problem of building a foreign-policy constituency. That organization's founders, including such distinguished Americans as the late Margaret Mead, Norman Cousins, Father Theodore Hesburgh, and former UN ambassador Charles Yost, expected the membership to reach 150,000 by the end of 1979. Despite the high hopes of its organizers, New Directions, whose dues-paying membership never exceeded 14,000, finally closed its doors in 1981.

Public apathy notwithstanding, the State Department would face another problem if it actively sought to build a "grass-roots" following. Section 14 of PL 93-126 (HR 7645) prohibits any use of appropriated funds for public-relations purposes. To its embarrassment the department was reminded of this in 1979 when it was admonished by Senator Dennis DeConcini (D.-N.M.) for using its personnel to lobby for inclusion of funds for the new Institute for Scientific and Technical Cooperation (ISTC) in the Foreign Operations Appropriations Bill (HR 4473). Prior to his committee's consideration of that measure, DeConcini had succeeded in securing floor approval of an amendment to drop ISTC from the Foreign Assistance Authorization Bill (HR 3324). But by the time that the Appropriations Committee took up the question of funding ISTC (which was still retained in House bills), DeConcini recognized that constituent pressure had been applied to several of his colleagues. Although twenty-one of twenty-eight Appropriations Committee members had supported his original floor amendment to HR 3324, enough of them switched their earlier held positions to defeat, on a tie vote, DeConcini's motion.

Subsequent investigation by Senate Appropriations Committee Chairman Warren Magnuson (D.-Wash.), during which the State Department reluctantly made its files available, revealed that the department had, in fact, acted to mobilize support for ISTC in various senators' home states. Having been burned once, the State Department will undoubtedly avoid any overt acts that might give rise to similar "whistle-blowing" episodes.[21]

Change the Constitution

In a provocative article in the fall 1980 issue of *Foreign Affairs*, Lloyd Cutler, counsel to President Carter, asserted that the virtues of the constitutional separation of powers were not without their costs. Cutler saw those costs mounting and suggested that they be examined to determine whether they could be reduced without losing the advantages of separation.

Cutler was attracted by the British-type parliamentary system in which "it is the duty of each majority member of the legislature to vote for each element of the Government's program, and the Government possesses the means to punish members if they do not. In a very real sense, each member's political future is tied to the fate of the Government his majority has formed. Politically speaking, he lives or dies by whether that Government lives or dies."

To enable our country to "form a Government," Cutler advocated "modest" constitutional changes which, he believed, would make our structure somewhat more like a parliamentary system, with somewhat less separation than now exists between the executive and legislative branches.

Cutler suggested that the Constitution be amended to "provide that in presidential election years, voters in each congressional district . . . be required to vote for a trio of candidates, as a team, for President, Vice President and the House of Representatives; . . . permit or require the President to select 50 percent of his Cabinet from among the members of his party in the Senate and House, who would retain their seats while serving in the Cabinet; [and] provide the President with the power, to be exercised not more than once in his term, to dissolve Congress and call for new congressional elections."[22]

As a "maverick" who has probably done as much as any politician to erode America's two-party system, I have come to recognize the policy paralysis that the decline of party discipline has fostered.* This, in part, explains why I changed parties after leaving Congress in 1979—the political scientist in me ultimately compelled me to move to a party whose views seem more compatible with mine. This concern for the deterioration of party responsibility also accounts for my growing appreciation for British-type democracy.

But I am a realist. If the House is unwilling to abide changes in committee jurisdiction, constitutional renovations that might diminish their electoral and policy independence would be anathema to the membership. Representatives who constantly outpoll their party's presidential candidates cannot be expected to embrace a plan that dismantles personal political machines that took many years to construct. Consequently, however meritorious Cutler's proposals, chances for their passage by the House in the form of a constitutional amendment resolution are remote.

Educate the Constituency

"All reforms," observed Richard Fenno, "carry costs—in this case an increased obligation of Congress's members to educate the people they represent."[23] But former Senator Fulbright complained that "the modern legislator, with some admirable exceptions, has discarded the role of education in favor of performing services for his constituents. . . . Furthermore, there has occurred a reversal of priorities between policy and politics. The responsible legislator will begin with a policy or program that he believes to be in the national

---

* Unquestionably, the gradual deterioration of American political parties has contributed to the atomization of the House of Representatives. As this is a separate subject in itself—ably analyzed by David Broder and others—it is not further explored here.

interest and then resort to technique and salesmanship to win its enactment. The new breed of Congressperson seems more inclined to test the market first to ascertain what is in current demand, and then to design a program to fit the market."[24]

While education is the one indispensable ingredient of representative government, many members ignore their responsibilities in that area. The complexity of present-day problems makes the kind of quick analysis that could be communicated to constituents difficult. Or, as a New Jersey Democrat said of one of his foreign-policy votes, "It would take a month of Sundays to explain it." Moreover, it often is more profitable, politically, to appeal to the public's baser instincts. In the same article in which he decried congresspersons' abandonment of their educational responsibilities, Fulbright professed not to see the fundamental importance of the poll tax, a position which mirrored the views of the people of his state on that issue.[25] That many of his constituents were being denied their constitutional right to vote did not seem to disturb Fulbright, a one-time associate professor of law at the University of Arkansas.

So while Fenno asked that individual members "work harder at their representational responsibilities—by explaining (to those they represent) their individual acts and the likely consequences of those acts for the collective performance of Congress,"[26] time and electoral pressures frequently conspire against such desirable conduct.

Evaluating the Proposals

While theoretically sound, most of these suggestions stand little chance of acceptance because they offend members' proprietary interests. Others, though, are already being pursued. As previously mentioned, the State Department's Office of Congressional Relations had increased its number of legislative management officers (LMOs) by 83 percent by 1980. Substitute amendments to neutralize troublesome amendments have become more common during floor proceedings. And some representatives still take their educational responsibilities seriously.

But these ten recommendations have two serious flaws. First, they disregard members' self-interests. With chiefs (148 committee and subcommittee chairmen) outnumbering Indians, the House is not likely to agree to proposals to subsume individual authority. Thus the consolidating of jurisdictions and the centralizing of decision making are not realistic possibilities. Second, the proposals fail to attack the mechanisms that create potential campaign problems, which, in turn, move legislators to actions to limit those dangers. Under these plans committee votes still would be a matter of record, and the ease with which floor amendment votes can be secured would not be constrained.

If it seems that I have been rather cavalier in my treatment of the ideas of a number of thoughtful students of the congressional scene, I must state that, having been a lawmaker for almost a quarter of a century and having worked, traveled, socialized, and prayed with hundreds of other solons, I believe I understand the thoughts, moods, aspirations, and eccentricities of legislators. These solutions simply do not recognize the human instincts and emotions that motivate members of the House of Representatives. Those who supported the futile efforts of the Bolling (1974), Obey (1977), and Patterson (1980) committees to achieve jurisdictional realignment can attest to this. Thus, I feel I would be raising false hopes by implying that these proposals, singly or in combination, would improve the House's performance in its foreign-policy deliberations.

A Proposal for a "Better" House

For some, a "reform of the reforms" is unnecessary, and they have effectively rationalized the troubles caused by "bad" foreign-policy votes. As Congressman Steve Solarz remarked at luncheon one day, "Chuck, maybe I have a vested interest in the institution, but, you know, the majority of the House's 'mistakes' in almost every instance have been reversed."[27] A review of the House's foreign-policy actions outlined in chapter 5 confirms Solarz's statement. Thanks to prodigious efforts by the executive branch and the House leadership, all but one either were dropped by the Senate or were repealed in subsequent sessions of Congress. My problem with this, of course, is that it permits much damage between the commission and the correction of the "mistake."

Others use history to assert that the pendulum of executive-legislative relations is already righting the imbalances that accompanied the reforms of the 1970s. By providing for a separation of powers, America's Founding Fathers established a system of government which operates most effectively in emergency situations, when executive-legislative concurrence becomes a necessity. As Thomas ("Tommy the Cork") Corcoran, one of Franklin Roosevelt's "Brain Trust," observed, "The only dynamic of democracy is catastrophe."[28] Our nation's history affords many examples of this, including the early hours of Roosevelt's New Deal. On March 9, 1933, during the first day of a special session called by the president, the House passed Roosevelt's Emergency Banking Bill armed only with the president's personal copy of this measure. No committee hearings were held, and Henry E. Steagall (D.-Ala.), chairman of the House Banking and Currency Committee, read the bill aloud in the chamber. Minority Leader Bert Snell (R.-N.Y.) brought the short debate to a close when he cried, "The house is burning down, and the President of the United States says this is the way to put out the fire. . . . I am going to give the President his way." The proposal was adopted unanimously by the House and approved later the same afternoon by the Senate.[29]

During its famous "Hundred Day" session in 1933, Congress also responded to a country pleading for answers to unemployment, bank closures, and dwindling crop prices by enacting the Agricultural Adjustment Act, the Farm Mortgage Act, the Tennessee Valley Authority, the Home Owners Loan Act, the National Industrial Recovery Act (which established the NRA), a $3.3-billion Public Works Administration Program, a $500-million Federal Emergency Relief Administration Program, new banking and securities legislation, an emergency Transportation Act, and the Civilian Conservation Corps.[30]

Seven years later, another "catastrophe," the war in Europe and Asia, prompted congressional imposition of our country's first peacetime draft. By the mid-1940s the Cold War crises, as Senator Fulbright suggested, produced quick legislative branch acceptance of the post–World War II foreign policy commitments outlined in chapter 2. Adoption of the massive National Defense Education Act in 1958 and Neil Armstrong's 1969 moon walk were attributable to the near hysteria created by the Soviets' October 4, 1957, launch of "Sputnik."

Federal legislators have supplicated themselves to the chief executive in times of crises because during national emergencies the citizenry turns to the president, not the Congress, for solutions. To ignore public concern in such situations is politically dangerous. As the crisis deepens, the congressional retreat accelerates. John Spanier and Eric Uslaner found that "the decision-making process of foreign policy questions appears to work best . . . when immediate and decisive action is required." In their book *How American Foreign Policy Is Made*, Spanier and Uslaner concluded that the "irony of foreign policy decision-making is . . . that the American political system appears to function best when decisions are made in the way authoritarian states formulate policies."[31]

But we should not need a major crisis to enable the House to achieve what James Sundquist termed "timely decisions. . . from a national viewpoint."[32] What is required is not another depression or World War III but, instead, modest refinements in House procedures. In the words of thirty-five House Democrats in their September 12, 1979, letter to Speaker O'Neill, the chamber's rules should be revamped to permit "a more rational approach to debates on the Floor of the House . . . to eliminate the frivolous, to streamline the process."[33]

Such modifications would not "roll back" the reforms of the 1970s if they conformed to four criteria. First, any rules revisions should preserve the committee, floor, and conference openness that presently exists in the House of Representatives. Second, procedural changes should be defensible against accusations that they are not philosophically attuned to the reforms of the last decade. Third, new procedures should not deny major constituent organizations the opportunity to have their legislative proposals considered on the House floor. Fourth, any alteration in current practices, while sensitive to the rights of individual members, should serve the overall public good.

In my judgment House adoption of the following three changes, all of which have been recommended at one time or another by member groups, would reduce the incidence of imprudent foreign-policy decisions without violating the spirit of the reforms of the 1970s. These revisions are not offered as a panacea. They would not eliminate friction between the two branches; the Constitution's "co-equal" provisions guarantee the perpetuation of presidential-congressional tensions. Nor would these suggestions necessarily heighten member responsibility. Rather, if instituted, *they would diminish the opportunity for irresponsibility.**

I propose, first, that rule 23, clause 2 (b) of the rules of the House of Representatives, which requires that "in the Committee of the Whole the chair shall order a recorded vote on request supported by at least *twenty-five* Members"[34] be changed to "*forty-four* Members." That would comport with rule 1, clause 5 (a), which requires that requests for a recorded vote when members are sitting in the House be supported by at least one-fifth (44) of a quorum (218). While not denying an individual the chance to offer a floor amendment, this suggestion does raise the question of a representative's "right" to a recorded vote. Personal and minority rights would be amply protected if 10 percent (44) of the body's 435 members were required to stand before a recorded tally could be ordered. The present 6-percent (25-member) requirement denigrates the amending process by failing to differentiate between what is important and what is unimportant. Any amendment, however mischievous, is practically guaranteed a recorded vote under current rules.

From a practical standpoint, the 44-standee proposal, if accepted by the House, probably would not curtail the introduction of amendments and the subsequent appeals for roll calls. Nevertheless, the difficulty in marshaling an additional 19 "requesters" would make it much more difficult for the sponsor to obtain a recorded vote, especially if the amendment had generated little constituent support in advance of its consideration (which is true of most of the foreign-policy amendments introduced during floor proceedings).

Second, the principle that prohibits legislation in an appropriations bill should be consistently applied. Rule 21, clause 2, proscribes expenditures for activities "not previously authorized by law." But it contains a loophole—the so-called Holman Rule—which makes in order amendments germane to the subject matter which "retrench expenditures by the reduction . . . of amounts of money covered by the bill."[35] This verbiage has been interpreted by successive House parliamentarians to permit restrictions not contained in any authorizing statute to be attached to appropriations measures.

To halt this jurisdictional encroachment, Representative Herbert

---

* These changes, of course, also would apply to the consideration and disposition of bills dealing with domestic policies and programs, with the same salutary results.

Harris (D.-Va.), on October 16, 1979, introduced H. Res. 446, which sought to prohibit any provision in an appropriations bill, or any amendment thereto, that changes existing law or imposes any limitation not contained in existing law. In a "Dear Colleague" letter, Harris wrote: "We simply cannot allow this abuse of the legislative process to continue. Appropriations bills should be money measures for purposes authorized by law—not Christmas trees on which to hang other unrelated issues."[36]

By invoking the Harris Resolution, the House would reduce the number of floor amendments that it otherwise would have to consider. In 1979, for example, 21.3 percent (33 of 155) of the foreign-policy amendments offered during floor debate were directed toward the Foreign Assistance Appropriations Bill (HR 4473). While the Harris approach would prohibit members from attaching restrictions to money measures, they would still have the opportunity to amend authorizing legislation. After all, the Nedzi-Whalen and Hamilton-Whalen "anti-Vietnam" efforts were aimed at the military procurement and foreign-assistance authorization bills, respectively.

Although forty-four fellow lawmakers joined Harris in cosponsoring H. Res. 446, the House failed to consider it during the Ninety-sixth Congress. However, on December 9, 1980, during the first meeting of Democrats elected to the Ninety-seventh Congress, the caucus debated this proposal and ultimately referred it to the Steering and Policy Committee for further study.

Third, as proposed by thirty-five Democrats on September 12, 1979, the House leadership should continue its "expansion of the use of the modified open rule"* to increase "the efficiency and quality of [the body's] work product."[37] In fact, reported Professor Bruce Oppenheimer, the House leadership has relied upon greater use of modified and closed rules to keep "the amending process and debate within boundaries, and to prevent Floor obstruction and the unravelling of legislation." Oppenheimer found that in the Ninety-fifth Congress (1977–78) over 20 percent (53 of 256) of all of the rules adopted by the House were modified open rules, compared to less than 1 percent (1 of 192) in the Ninetieth Congress (when amendment votes were not recorded).

Oppenheimer further discovered that closed or modified rules

---

* A "modified open rule" is one which limits the introduction of amendments during floor proceedings to those specified in the rule. No other amendments are in order.

were most often invoked for those pieces of legislation considered important to the leadership.[38] There were several such examples in the Ninety-sixth Congress. In July 1979 the House debated the Trade Agreements Act (HR 4537) under a closed rule. In their article in *The World Economy*, I. M. Destler and Thomas R. Graham concluded that the way in which HR 4537 was handled reassured those abroad that America's constitutional system can work on foreign-policy issues: "What the Legislature enacted was consistent with what the Executive negotiated."[39] On November 2, 1979, the House withstood a Republican challenge to open a major welfare reform bill (HR 4904) to amendment. The House Rules Committee, on April 17, 1980, brought to the floor a rule permitting only eight amendments to the First Budget Resolution for fiscal 1981.

Oppenheimer expressed the belief that reliance on the modified rule will continue to grow. Many members privately welcome the opportunity it affords to escape taking positions on controversial amendments. Its application, however, must be judicious. Failure to grant important interest groups their "day in court" must be avoided. The House leadership learned this lesson the hard way in July–August 1980 when, desiring to keep the lid on federal spending, it requested the Rules Committee to limit to two (both non-controversial) the number of floor amendments that could be offered to the Budget Reconciliation Bill (HR 7765). But in the face of strong pressure from civil-service and military retirees, three Rules Committee Democrats—Joe Moakley (Mass.), Shirley Chisholm (N.Y.), and Leo Zeferetti (N.Y.)—insisted on permitting a House vote on a motion to restore the semiannual cost-of-living pension adjustment,* which, in an effort to save $750 million, the Budget Committee had deleted in its mark-up of HR 7765. The heretical Democrats held out for more than a month, finally forcing Speaker O'Neill to acquiesce to their demands. The Rules Commit-

---

* To compensate for inflation federal retirees formerly received an annual adjustment to their pensions. While this permitted an end-of-the-year "catch-up," pensioners' buying power, during the course of the year, eroded considerably. To enable them to recoup this loss, Congress enacted legislation providing retirees an additional 1 percent in pension benefits (over and above the cost-of-living adjustment). This 1-percent "kicker," when eliminated by Congress in 1976, was replaced by a semiannual adjustment provision. This semiannual adjustment, however, was eliminated when Congress, in 1981, restored the original once-a-year adjustment provision.

tee made consideration of the amendment in order, and when offered by Representative Bauman on September 4, 1980, it easily passed the House, 309–72.

The Rules Committee is much less likely to encounter such organized resistance to regulations restricting floor amendments on foreign-policy measures. I cannot recall receiving one constituent communication, pro or con, *in advance* of the introduction of the foreign-policy amendments discussed in chapter 5. (My mail on the Turkish arms sale came after passage of the embargo amendment.) Unconcerned about the minutiae of our international relations, the average American was simply unaware of them. These amendments became issues only after the vote, when they were exploited by those seeking to create emotional antiincumbent campaign themes.

Of course, individual congressmen may cry "gag" when debate is limited by a closed or modified open rule. On October 19, 1979, for example, Representative John Ashbrook decried the rule proposed for HR 4904, the welfare-reform bill.

> One of the things I would remind my friends on the other side of the aisle since my memory goes back a few years, I remember when some of my liberal friends were trying to get votes, one on the Nedzi-Whalen amendment to end the Vietnam war; and, two on [a Whalen amendment] to vote directly on the draft. There were people on our side of the aisle even though we opposed these amendments, who were working with you and voting against restrictive rules that up to that point made it impossible for you to get a vote [on these] amendments. It is a strange sword that cuts both ways and I think we should worry about how that sword cuts before the rules are changed and the opportunity for amendment unduly restricted.[40]

Complaints such as Ashbrook's could be deflected by imposing a modified open rule that provided for floor consideration of only those amendments that had previously been submitted to the committee of jurisdiction during its mark-up of the bill. Such a rule would serve several purposes. It would preserve the author's right to present the amendment during floor debate, but by mandating that the amendment first be heard in committee, the rule would afford the occasion for a thorough review by committee members and administration officials. All of the relevant facts would then be available during floor proceedings. Most important, however, this and other types of modified open rules would, according to the thirty-five Democrats, "serve the common good [by recognizing] the needs of the institution itself."[41]

Effects of the Proposed Procedural Changes

The three-point program advanced here is a practical one in that it encompasses proposals that already have considerable backing in the House of Representatives. Thus, prospects for its implementation are much better than for the suggestions reviewed earlier in this chapter.

The modification of House rules and practices to accommodate these three recommendations would have several effects. By forbidding legislation on appropriations bills and expanding the use of closed or modified open rules, these procedural revisions would greatly diminish the number of foreign- as well as domestic-policy amendments that the House would have to consider. Increasing from twenty-five to forty-four the number necessary to obtain a roll call would reduce the number of amendments for which recorded votes would be ordered. This reduction in the number of recorded votes would benefit both the leadership and the members—the former by strengthening its capacity to control the flow of legislation; the latter by limiting exposure to politically damaging votes. Finally, better foreign policy would emerge from institutional changes that restrict opportunities to offer amendments harmful to our national interests, enhance the legislative powers of the House leadership, and minimize the need for members to take measures to limit possible electoral damage.

Conclusion

House reforms of the last decade must be placed in historical perspective. They are procedural reforms and, as such, must not be confused with legislation itself. In the year 2000 the House of the 1970s will be judged by historians and political scientists not on its procedural changes but on its legislative record. Reviewing 1971, for example, congressional chroniclers will mark that as the year in which the House ended plans to develop an American supersonic transport aircraft. That this was the House's first opportunity to go on record concerning the SST probably will earn little more than a footnote.

To keep these reforms within their proper frame of reference, other points must be borne in mind. First, the "decade of reform" was only incidental to, not the cause of, the executive-legislative conflicts of the 1970s. White House–congressional feuds date from the first Congress in 1789. As early as 1818, President Monroe complained that "the late session [of Congress], considering the flourishing and happy condition of the country, has been unusually oppressive on the Executive Department. . . . A very querulous spirit has been manifested."[42]

Second, presidential excesses were the cause, House reforms the result, of congressional indignation. All of the evidence strongly supports the theory that one of the House's principal purposes in drafting new procedures was to equip itself with more effective tools with which to cope with an aggressive presidency.

Third, in establishing new rules during the 1970s, House reformers were able to achieve their three goals—decentralization of power, greater openness, and enhanced ability to deal with the executive—thereby breaching the policymaking barriers outlined in chapter 1. In so doing, however, they did nothing to improve the chamber's legislative performance or efficiency. In fact, the House's capacity for rational decision-making has been weakened by its new processes—the power of House leaders has waned, and representatives feel increasingly exposed to, and fearful of, constituent recriminations and have become more likely to make committee and floor votes that limit the possibilities for damage in later elections.

By invoking procedural changes along the lines that I have proposed, it should be possible to halt and reverse that erosion. But while such revisions would improve the House's international-affairs record, they would be too narrow in scope to end that body's dependence upon the executive branch for foreign-policy initiatives and direction. The House's role would continue to be that of the reviewer and modifier.

Drawing on the Augustinian definition of sin ("the absence of good"), one might say that good foreign policy is often the absence of bad decisions. State Department officials have already acknowledged that congressional inquisitiveness in foreign-policy matters has made precipitous actions in a crisis less likely. Thus, the legislative strictures of the 1970s may have discouraged the chief executive from committing massive arms shipments and military personnel to such trouble spots as Angola, Zaire's Shaba Province, and the Ogaden region in the Horn of Africa. It is this capacity of House reforms to prevent possible recurrence of past presidential "tyrannies" that has proved most useful.

But the price has been great. While diminishing potential misadventures by the executive branch, the House's new operational methods have often bred legislative excesses and contributed to House actions that have repudiated long-standing global obligations, threatened the continued existence of several international organizations, and offended many friendly nations in both hemispheres.

The United States cannot afford to stand alone in an interdependent world. This is why it is imperative that the House improve its foreign-policy efforts. A significant step in that direction would be the adoption of measures that would, simultaneously, reduce the number of recorded votes on amendments, thereby minimizing the margin for error, strengthen the House leadership, and permit members to vote more dispassionately on foreign-policy bills and amendments. The three rules modifications that I have suggested, which already enjoy considerable member support, offer the House its best hope for achieving those ends.

Appendix: Tables

☆　☆　☆　☆　☆

Table 1. Bills for Which Foreign Affairs Committee Had Sole Jurisdiction (1979)

Bill Number	Origin	Referral	Subcommittee Action
HR 2479 U.S.-Taiwan Relations Act	presidential draft bill sent to Congress on 1/26/79	Subcommittee on Asian and Pacific Affairs	hearings only
HR 3324 International Development Cooperation Act of 1979	presidential draft bill sent to Congress on 2/28/79	various sub-committees	hearings and recommendations to full committee
HR 3173 International Security Assistance Act of 1979	message from secretary of state, accompanied by a draft bill, sent to Congress on 2/23/79	various sub-committees	hearings and recommendations to full committee
HR 4035 Special International Security Assistance Act of 1979	presidential letter, 4/2/79; presidential draft bill, 4/9/79	Subcommittees on International Security and Scientific Affairs; Europe and the Middle East	hearings and mark-up; two minor amendments
HR 3363 Dept. of State, ICA, and Board for International Broadcasting Authorization Act for 1980 and 1981	Executive Communication 569 containing draft legislation	Subcommittee on International Operations	hearings and mark-up
HR 2774 Arms Control and Disarmament Act Authorization	Executive Communication 860 containing draft legislation	Subcommittee on International Security and Scientific Affairs	hearings and mark-up; approved by full committee without amendment
HR 4034 Export Administration Act Amendments of 1979	executive-branch proposal containing draft legislation	Subcommittee on International Economic Policy and Trade	hearings and mark-up

Table 1. *continued*

Bill Number	Origin	Referral	Subcommittee Action
HR 4955 Authorizing Additional Appropriations for Migration and Refugee Assistance	Executive Communication 2123 containing draft legislation	Subcommittee on International Operations	hearings and mark-up
HR 3897 Removing Uganda Prohibitions		Subcommittee on Africa	hearings and mark-up
HR 5279 ICA Agency Film "Reflections: George Meany"		full committee	
HR 3956 Consent to Accept Honorary Counsel Hewson Ryan		Subcommittee on International Operations	requested report from State Department
HR 5079 International Energy Exposition		Subcommittee on International Economic Policy and Trade	hearings and mark-up
HR 5218 Caribbean Disaster Assistance		full committee	
HR 4439 Sanctions against Zimbabwe and Rhodesia	presidential announcement, 6/7/79	full committee	

Source: U.S., Congress, House of Representatives, Foreign Affairs Committee, 96th Congress, *Survey of Activities,* pp. 19–46.

Table 2. Floor Action—1969 Foreign-Policy Bills

Bill	Description	Date of House Action	Committee Jurisdiction	Floor Manager	House Action	Total Amendments Offered	Total Amendments Approved	Amendments Offered by Noncommittee Members	Noncommittee Amendments Approved
HR 33	Increasing Participation of the U.S. in the International Development Assn.	3/12/69	Banking and Currency	chairman	passed, 247–150	0	0	0	0
HR 3666	Immigration and Nationality Act Extension	6/16/69	Judiciary	subcom. chairman	passed, consent	0	0	0	0
HR 12964	State Justice and Commerce Depts Appropriations, FY 1970	7/24/69	Appropriations	subcom. chairman	passed, 366–31	0	0	0	0
HR 12829	Interest Equalization Tax Extension Act of 1969	8/7/69	Ways and Means	chairman	passed, voice	0	0	0	0
HR 4813	Extension of U.S. Fishing Fleet Investment Act	8/12/69	Merchant Marine and Fisheries	subcom. chairman	passed, voice	1	1	1	1
HR 11039	Peace Corps Act Amendment 1969	9/8/69	Foreign Affairs	chairman	passed, 281–52	2	1	0	0
HR	International Claims	10/6/69	Foreign	chairman	passed,	0	0	0	0

Bill	Title	Date	Committee	Status				
HR 14580	Foreign Assistance Act of 1969	11/20/69	Foreign Affairs	chairman	passed, 176–163	25[†]	11	8	4
HRes 613	Toward Peace with Justice Res.	12/2/69	Foreign Affairs	subcom. chairman	passed, 334–55	0[‡]	0	0	0
HR 15149	FY 1970 Foreign Aid Appropriations	12/9/69	Appropriations	subcom. chairman	passed, 200–195	9	3	7	2
HR 14789	Foreign Service Act Annuities Adjustment	12/15/69	Foreign Affairs	subcom. chairman	passed, voice	0	0	0	0
SJR 90	Proposed International Conference on a Patent Cooperation Treaty	12/15/69	Foreign Affairs	subcom. chairman	passed, voice	0	0	0	0
HCon Res 454	Calling for Humane Treatment and Release of American POWs	12/15/69	Foreign Affairs	subcom. chairman	passed, 405–0	0	0	0	0
Totals						44	18	19	7

* No amendment offered to the State Department title.
[†] Does not include amendments correcting printing errors.
[‡] Closed rule—Recommittal motion adopted, 392–0.

Source: U.S., Congress, *Congressional Record*, 91st Congress, 1st session (dates on which fourteen bills were debated).

Table 3. Floor Action—1979 Foreign-Policy Bills

Bill	Description	Date of House Action	Committee Jurisdiction	Floor Manager	House Action	Total Amendments Offered	Total Amendments Approved	Amendments Offered by Noncommittee Members	Noncommittee Amendments Approved
HR 1147	Duty Waiver Extension	3/1/79	Ways and Means	chairman	passed, voice	0	0	0	0
HR 2974	Taiwan Relations	3/13/79	Foreign Affairs	chairman	passed, 345–55	23	11	14	4
HR 2774	Arms Control and Disarmament Agency	3/22/79	Foreign Affairs	chairman	passed, 296–100	3	2	1	0
HR 3173	Foreign Military Aid Authorization	3/29/79	Foreign Affairs	chairman	passed, voice	2	2	1	1
HR 3324	Foreign Aid Authorization	4/10/79	Foreign Affairs	chairman	passed, 220–173	27	20	17	11
HR 3363	State Department Authorization	4/24/79	Foreign Affairs	subcom. chairman	passed, 256–146	7	6	5	4
HR 3897	Aid to Uganda	5/21/79	Foreign Affairs	subcom. chairman	passed, voice	0	0	0	0
HR 4035	Special Aid to Egypt and Israel	5/30/79	Foreign Affairs	subcom. chairman	passed, 347–28	3	3	3	3
HR 111	Panama Canal Treaty Implementation	6/21/79	4 House committees	3 committee chairmen; 1 subcom. chairman	passed, 224–202	21	14	6	3
HR	200-mile Fishing	6/25/79	Merchant	subcom.	passed,	0	0	0	0

Bill	Title	Date	Committee	Role	Vote				
HR 4537	Trade Act of 1979	7/11/79	Ways and Means	chairman	passed, 395–7	0	0	0	0
HRes 231	Disapproval Res. Foreign Aid Reorganization	7/11/79	Government Operations	chairman	defeated, 156–256*	0	0	0	0
HR 4392	State, Justice, Commerce Appro.	7/12/79	Appropriations	subcom. chairman	passed, 299–93	4	3	1	1
HR 3956	Hewson A. Ryan Consulate Approv.	7/16/79	Foreign Affairs	subcom. chairman	passed, voice	0	0	0	0
HRes 317	Romanian Emigration Disapproval Res.	7/25/79	Ways and Means	subcom. chairman	defeated, 126–271†	0	0	0	0
HR 4473	Foreign Aid Appropriation	9/6/79	Appropriations	subcom. chairman	passed, 224–183	33	22	12	7
HR 5279	ICA Film "George Meany"	9/24/79	Foreign Affairs	chairman	passed, voice	0	0	0	0
HR 5218	Caribbean Disaster Assistance	9/25/79	Foreign Affairs	chairman	passed, 370–27	0	0	0	0
HR 4034	Export Control Extension	9/25/79	Foreign Affairs	subcom. chairman	passed, voice	1	0	1	0
HR 5163	Sale of Naval Ships Abroad	9/25/79	Armed Services	subcom. chairman	passed, 232–22	0	0	0	0
HR 5079	International Energy Exposition	10/9/79	Foreign Affairs	chairman	passed, voice	0	0	0	0
HR 2172	Sugar Support Bill	10/23/79	Agriculture	chairman	defeated, 158–249	8	6	8	6

Table 3. *continued*

Bill	Description	Date of House Action	Committee Jurisdiction	Floor Manager	House Action	Total Amendments Offered	Total Amendments Approved	Amendments Offered by Noncommittee Members	Noncommittee Amendments Approved
HR 4955	Add'l Author. Migrants and Immigration	10/25/79	Foreign Affairs	subcom. chairman	passed, 301–69	1	1	0	0
HRes 428	Disapproval Res. Trade Reogan.	11/8/79	Government Operations	chairman	defeated, voice‡	0	0	0	0
HJR 440	Continuing Appropriations Indo-China Refugees	11/13/79	Appropriations	chairman	passed, voice	2	1	2	1
HR 2727	Meat Import Quota	11/14/79	Ways and Means	chairman	passed, 352–48	4	2	0	0
HR 5580	NATO Mutual Support Act	12/3/79	Foreign Affairs; Armed Serv.	subcom. chairman	passed, voice	0	0	0	0
HR 4865	Elephant Protection Act	12/19/79	Referred to 3 committees	chairman	passed, voice	0	0	0	0
HR 2816	Refugee Act of 1979	12/20/79	Judiciary	subcom. chairman	passed, 328–47	15	11	4	4
Totals						155	104	75	45

*Defeat of disapproval resolution resulted in House approval of president's reorganization plan.

†Defeat of disapproval resolution resulted in House approval of president's Romanian emigration declaration.

‡Defeat of disapproval resolution resulted in House approval of president's reorganization plan.

Source: U.S. Congress, *Congressional Record*, 96th Congress, 1st session (dates on which thirty bills were debated).

Table 4. Reelection Success of House Incumbents

Year	Members Seeking Reelection	Defeated Primary	Defeated General	Percent Reelected
1960	405	5*	25	92.6
1962	402	12	22	91.5
1964	397	8	45	86.6
1966	411	8	41	88.1
1968	409	4	9	96.8
1970	401	10	12	94.5
1972	390	12†	13	93.6
1974	391	8	40	87.7
1976	384	3	13	95.8
1978	382	5	19	93.7
1980	398	6	32	90.4

*Does not include Harold B. McSween (D.-La.), who was defeated in the primary by Earl K. Long, who died before the general election. McSween replaced Long on the November ballot and was elected to another term.

†The higher than usual number of primary defeats results from decennial Congressional redistricting, which placed two incumbents in the same new district.

Sources: 1960–1978 Elections, *Congressional Quarterly Weekly Report* (Washington: Congressional Quarterly, Inc., April 5, 1980), p. 908; 1980 Elections. *Congressional Quarterly Weekly Report* (Washington: Congressional Quarterly, Inc., November 8, 1980), pp. 3338–45.

Notes

CHAPTER 1

1. U.S., Congress, House, *Congressional Record*, 95th Cong., 1st sess., Jan. 12, 1977, p. H33.

2. "Kissinger on Oil, Food and Trade," *Business Week*, Jan. 13, 1975, p. 73.

3. Hon. Charles W. Whalen, Jr., *Washington Post*, Aug. 24, 1974, p. A18.

4. Thomas M. Franck and Edward Weisband, *Foreign Policy by Congress* (New York: Oxford University Press, 1979), p. 3.

5. William D. Rogers, "Who's in Charge of Foreign Policy?" *New York Times Magazine*, Sept. 9, 1979, p. 49.

CHAPTER 2

1. U.S., Congress, House, Committee on International Relations, *Special Subcommittee on Investigation (Hamilton Committee) Report*, Jan. 2, 1977.

2. Ralph K. Huitt, "Congress: The Durable Partner," in *Congress and the President: Allies and Adversaries*, ed. Ronald C. Moe (California: Goodyear Publishing Company, 1971), p. 304.

3. John S. Saloma III, *Congress and the New Politics* (Boston: Little, Brown, 1969), p. 30.

4. Woodrow Wilson, *Congressional Government* (Cleveland: Meridian Books, 1969), p. 31.

5. Ibid., p. 196.

6. Ibid., p. 22.

7. Stephen D. Cohen, *The Making of United States International Economic Policy: Principles, Proposals for Reform* (New York: Praeger, 1977), p. 7.

8. Ibid., p. 7.

9. J. William Fulbright, "Congress and Foreign Policy," in *Congress and the President*, p. 198.

10. *Public Papers of the Presidents of the United States: Harry S. Truman, 1947* (Washington, D.C.: Office of Federal Registrar, 1963–), pp. 178–79.

11. Ibid., *1948*, p. 185.

12. Ibid., *1950*, p. 492.

13. Statistics given by Defense Department personnel from "US Military Strength Sheet," *Facts of the World*, Nov. 18, 1980.

14. Robert Murphy, *Diplomat among Warriors* (Garden City, N.Y.: Doubleday, 1964), pp. 408–9.

15. *Public Papers of the Presidents of the United States: Lyndon B. Johnson, 1965* (Washington, D.C.: Office of Federal Registrar, 1966), 1: 593–96.

16. *Johnson Presidential Papers, 1965*, p. 293.

17. Author's meeting with President Johnson in the White House, Aug. 17, 1967.

18. *Public Papers of the Presidents of the United States: Richard M. Nixon, 1970* (Washington, D.C.: Office of Federal Registrar, 1971), p. 406.

19. Alfred Steinberg, *Sam Rayburn* (New York: Hawthorn, 1975), pp. 179–80, 188.

20. Lee H. Hamilton and Michael Van Dusen, "Making the Separation of Powers Work," *Foreign Affairs* 57 (fall 1978): 17–39.

21. Senator John Jackson Sparkman, "Checks and Balances in American Foreign Policy," *Indiana Law Journal* 52 (winter 1977): 434.

22. Neil Sheehan et al., *The Pentagon Papers: The Secret History of the Vietnam War* (New York: Quadrangle, 1971), p. 246.

23. George H. Gallup, *The Gallup Poll: Public Opinion, 1972–1975* (Wilmington, Del.: Scholarly Resources, 1978), 1: 101, 138, 154, 206.

24. Ibid., p. 87.

25. George H. Gallup, *Gallup Poll, 1935–1971* (New York: Random House, 1972), 3: 1921.

26. Gallup, *Gallup Poll, 1972–1975*, p. 119.

27. Ibid., pp. 113, 207, 210.

28. Ibid., p. 210.

29. Norman J. Ornstein, *Congress in Change: Evolution and Reform* (New York: Praeger, 1975), p. 89.

30. Eugene Eidenberg and Roy D. Morey, *An Act of Congress: The Legislative Process and the Making of Education Policy* (New York: Norton, 1969), p. 36.

31. U.S., Congress, House, Republican Policy Committee, *Statement on Congressional Reorganization*, May 10, 1967, p. 1.

32. U.S., Congress, House, Democratic Study Group, 95th Cong., 2nd sess., *Special Report: Reform in the House of Representatives*, no. 95-18 (Nov. 6, 1978), p. 4.

CHAPTER 3

1. U.S., Congress, House Democratic Caucus, 96th Cong., 1st sess., *Preamble and Rules*, sec. M1. D, p. 3.

2. Richard Bolling, *Power in the House* (New York: Dutton, 1968), p. 41.

3. Ibid.

4. Lewis A. Froman, Jr., *The Congressional Process: Strategies, Rules and Procedures* (Boston: Little, Brown, 1967), p. 217.

5. House Democratic Caucus, *Preamble and Rules*, p. 3.

6. Ibid., sec. M2. B, p. 4.

7. Ibid., sec. M5. A, p. 4.

8. Ibid., p. 5.

9. Ibid., sec. M2. B, p. 4.

10. Ibid., sec. M3. A, p. 4.

11. Ibid., sec. M5. B, p. 5.

12. Ibid., sec. M3. A, p. 4.

13. "Committee Secrecy," *Congressional Quarterly Almanac,* 1970 (Washington, D.C.: Congressional Quarterly Press, 1971), p. 1117.

14. U.S., Congress, House, Republican Policy Committee, *Statement on Congressional Reorganization,* May 10, 1967, p. 1.

15. American Federation of Labor and Congress of Industrial Organizations, "Congressional Reform," statement made at the 1963 convention, p. 67.

16. *Congressional Quarterly Weekly Report,* April 7, 1979, p. 637.

17. U.S., Congress, House, Democratic Study Group, 95th Cong., 2nd sess., *Special Report: Reform in the House of Representatives,* no. 95-18 (Nov. 6, 1978), p. 5.

18. John W. Kingdon, *Congressmen's Voting Decisions* (New York: Harper and Row, 1973), p. 120.

19. U.S., Congress, House, Democratic Study Group, *Special Report: Secrecy in the House of Representatives,* June 24, 1970, p. 7.

20. U.S., Congress, House, *Congressional Record,* 91st Cong., 2nd sess., July 27, 1970, H25797.

21. CBS, transcript for "Sixty Minutes," vol. 3, no. 17 (May 11, 1971).

22. U.S., Congress, House, *Congressional Record,* 92nd Cong., 2nd sess., Feb. 8, 1972, pp. H3202–3.

23. Ibid.

24. Stephen E. Frantzich, "The Over Time Pattern of Innovation among Members of the House of Representatives," paper delivered to the Midwest Political Science Association in Chicago, April 1980, p. 6.

25. Ibid., p. 7.

26. Ibid., p. 8.

27. Congressional Research Service, Foreign Affairs Division, *Background Information on the Use of Armed Forces in Foreign Countries* (Washington, D.C.: Government Printing Office, 1975), pp. 58–66.

28. Louis Fisher, *President and Congress: Power and Policy* (New York: Free Press, 1973), p. 175.

29. Ibid., p. 200.

30. Ibid., p. 204.

31. PL 93-148, *War Powers Act,* 1973.

32. Cecil V. Crabb, Jr., and Pat M. Holt, *Invitation to Struggle: Congress, the President, and Foreign Policy* (Washington, D.C.: Congressional Quarterly Press, 1980), p. 46.

33. *Public Papers of the Presidents of the United States: Richard M. Nixon, 1973* (Washington, D.C.: Office of Federal Registrar, 1975), p. 36.

34. Josel Havemann, *Congress and the Budget* (Bloomington: Indiana University Press, 1978), p. 177.

35. U.S., Congress, Senate, Judiciary Committee, Subcommittee on the Separation of Powers, Subcommittee Hearing, Mar. 24, 1974.

36. PL 93-344, *Congressional Budget Act,* June 18, 1974.

37. Havemann, *Congress*, p. 174.

38. Ibid., p. 15.

39. U.S., Congress, House, Foreign Affairs Committee, *Report on HR 17234, Foreign Assistance Act of 1974*, Oct. 24, 1974, pp. 48–49.

40. Ibid.

41. Ibid.

42. Ibid.

43. Ibid.

44. Ibid.

45. Ibid.

46. Ibid.

47. Ibid.

48. Ibid.

49. Ibid.

50. Ibid., pp. 41–42.

51. Ibid.

52. PL 95-148, *Foreign Aid Appropriations*, 1977.

53. U.S., Congress, House, *Congressional Record*, 96th Cong., 1st sess., Dec. 31, 1979, p. H12522.

CHAPTER 4

1. Personal interview, July 1, 1980

2. U.S., Congress, *Congressional Record: Daily Digest*, 91st Cong., 1st sess., Dec. 23, 1969, p. D669.

3. Ibid., 96th Cong., 1st sess., Jan. 3, 1980, p. D1769.

4. Burdett A. Loomis, "The 'Me' Decade and the Changing Context of the House Leadership," paper delivered at E. Dirksen Conference, "Understanding Congressional Leadership," Washington, June 10–11, 1980, p. 14.

5. "Characteristics of the 96th Congress," *Congressional Quarterly Almanac*, 1979, p. 5.

6. "Conservative Coalition Voting Studies," *Congressional Quarterly Almanac*, 1979, pp. 34C–39C.

7. "House Conservative Coalition: 1969 and 90th Congress," *Congressional Quarterly Almanac*, 1969, pp. 1058–59.

8. U.S., Congress, House, Democratic Study Group, 95th Cong., 2nd sess., *Special Report: Reform in the House of Representatives*, no. 95-18 (Nov. 6, 1978), p. 5.

9. Loomis, "'Me' Decade," p. 14.

10. Lawrence C. Dodd and Bruce I. Oppenheimer, "The House in Transition," in *Congress Reconsidered*, ed. Lawrence C. Dodd and Bruce I. Oppenheimer (New York: Praeger, 1976), p. 39.

11. U.S., Congress, House, Committee on Foreign Affairs, 96th Cong., 1st sess., *Survey of Activities* (Washington, D.C.: Government Printing Office, 1980), pp. 1–4.

12. A record of the House debate on HR 6942 appears in the *Congressional Record*, 96th Cong., 2nd sess., June 5, 1980, pp. H4537–H4600.

13. Personal interview, June 20, 1978.

14. Leroy N. Rieselback, *Congressional System: Notes and Readings*, 2nd ed. (N. Scituate, Mass.: Duxbury Press, 1979), p. 399.

15. Foreign Affairs Committee, *Survey of Activities*, 1980, pp. 19–47.

16. Ibid., p. 158.

17. "Committee Secrecy," *Congressional Quarterly Almanac*, 1975, p. 932.

18. Foreign Affairs Committee, *Survey of Activities*, 1980, p. 158.

19. Ibid., 91st Cong., 2nd sess., pp. 4–7.

20. Ibid., 96th Cong., pp. 4–7.

21. Telephone interview with representative of the Office of the Official Reporters, July 22, 1980.

22. Hon. Charles W. Whalen, Jr., *Congressional Record*, Mar. 21, 1971, p. H7571.

23. U.S., Congress, House, 96th, 2nd session, *Continuation of Hearings before Subcommittee on Treasury, U.S. Postal Service Appropriations*, Mar. 17, 1980. Statement by Robert Rota, attachment.

24. Stephen E. Frantzich, "Over Time Pattern of Innovation among Members of the House of Representatives," paper delivered to the Midwest Political Science Association in Chicago, April 1980, pp. 7–8.

25. Norman Ornstein, "Is Congress Too Good for Us?" *Washington Post*, Nov. 18, 1979, p. C5.

26. U.S., Congress, House, Hearings before Subcommittee on International Security and Scientific Affairs, 94th Cong., 1st sess., *War Powers: A Test of Compliance*, May 7 and June 4, 1975, p. v.

27. U.S., Congress, House, *Congressional Oversight of War Powers Compliance: Zaire Airlift*, Hearing before Subcommittee on International Security and Scientific Affairs, Aug. 10, 1978, pp. 28–29.

28. *Congressional Quarterly Weekly Report*, May 3, 1980, p. 1194.

29. Martin Tolchin, "Congress Broadens Its Influence on Foreign Policy," *New York Times*, Dec. 24, 1979, p. A9.

30. Ibid.

31. George H. Gallup, *The Gallup Poll: Public Opinion, 1972–1975* (Wilmington, Del.: Scholarly Resources, 1978), 3:519.

32. Gallup Polling Service, telephone interviews, April 26, 27, 1980.

33. Tolchin, "Congress Broadens," p. A9.

34. Fiscal Year 1979 figure, telephone interview with spokesman for Department of Defense, Aug. 1, 1980.

35. "Reagan Rallies Bipartisan AWACs Support as Haig Cautions Hill," *Washington Post*, Oct. 6, 1981, p. A22.

36. U.S., Congress, House, 96th Cong., *International Security and Development (Foreign Aid Authorization) Bill*, HR 6942, sec. 662.

37. Personal interview with Robert Flaten, Mar. 21, 1980.

38. Ibid.

39. Douglas J. Bennet, "Congress in Foreign Policy: Who Needs It?" *Foreign Affairs* 57 (fall 1978): 40–50.

40. Tolchin, "Congress Broadens," p. A9.

41. Leonard Downie, Jr., "North-South Economic Talks Stalled 6 Months After Brandt Group's Plea," *Washington Post*, July 19, 1980, p. 14.

42. Christopher J. Deering and Steven S. Smith, "Majority Party Leadership and the Effect of Decentralization," paper delivered at E. Dirksen Conference, "Under-

standing Congressional Leadership," Washington, June 11, 1980, p. 39.

43. Randall B. Ripley, *Majority Party Leadership in Congress* (Boston: Little, Brown, 1969), p. 8.

44. Paul Clancy and Shirley Elder, *Tip: A Biography of Thomas P. "Tip" O'Neill, Speaker of the House* (New York: Macmillan, 1980), p. 111.

45. Personal interview with John Brademas (D.-Ind.), June 24, 1980.

46. Robert L. Peabody, Jeffery M. Berry, William G. Frasure, and Jerry Goldman. *To Enact a Law: Congress and Campaign Financing* (New York: Praeger, 1972), p. 128.

47. Personal interview with Joseph McCaffrey, congressional correspondent, radio station WMAL, June 18, 1980.

48. Roger H. Davidson and Walter Oleszek, *Congress against Itself* (Bloomington: Indiana University Press, 1977), p. 16.

CHAPTER 5

1. U.S., Congress, House, Democratic Study Group, 95th Cong., 2nd sess., *Special Report: Reform in the House of Representatives*, no. 95-18 (Nov. 6, 1978), p. 8.

2. Dean Acheson, *Present at the Creation: My Years in the State Department* (New York, Norton, 1969), p. 674.

3. U.S., Congress, House, Committee on International Relations, 94th Cong., 2nd sess., *Congress and Foreign Policy*, Hearings before the Special Subcommittee (Hamilton Committee) on Investigations, prepared statement by Roger H. Davidson, June 17, 1976, p. 10.

4. Cecil V. Crabb, Jr., and Pat M. Holt, *Invitation to Struggle: Congress, the President, and Foreign Policy* (Washington, D.C.: Congressional Quarterly Press, 1980), p. 35.

5. Charles O. Jones, "Will Reform Change Congress?" in *Congress Reconsidered*, ed. Lawrence C. Dodd and Bruce I. Oppenheimer (New York: Praeger, 1976), p. 250.

6. Hamilton Subcommittee on Investigations, *Congress and Foreign Policy*, July 22, 1976, p. 192.

7. James A. Robinson, *Congress and Foreign Policy Making* (Homewood, Illinois: Dorsey Press, 1967), p. 56.

8. David S. Truman, *The Governmental Process* (New York: Knopf, 1951), p. 423.

9. Edward Bruske, "The Making of an Issue," *Washington Post*, Oct. 21, 1980, pp. C1, C3.

10. "House Reform," *The Economist*, Oct. 19–25, 1974, p. 73.

11. "The Bretton Woods Proposals: Message of President Roosevelt to Congress," *Department of State Bulletin* 12, no. 295 (Feb. 12, 1945): 220, 221, 222.

12. Edmund Muskie, "Congress Jeopardizing Policy by Not Approving Aid Bill," *Washington Post*, June 14, 1980, p. A11.

13. Bailey Morse, "U.S. Hurt by Its Failure to Fund Development Agencies," *Washington Star*, Sept. 24, 1980, p. E1.

14. Hon. W. Henson Moore, *Congressional Record*, June 23, 1977, pp. H20595–96.

15. Palm oil statistics have been compiled from several letters and memoranda from the International Bank for Reconstruction and Development dated 1976 and 1977.

16. "The Bank and the Wreckers," editorial, *Washington Post*, Oct. 8, 1979, p. A20.

17. Frank Trippitt, "The Down and Ups of Foreign Aid," *Time*, Mar. 26, 1979, p. 48.

18. "A Bargain at Any Price," *Journal of Commerce and Commercial*, April 5, 1979, p. 4.

19. "McNamara Censured for Political Acts," *Los Angeles Times*, Dec. 10, 1979, p. 15.

20. James Srodes, "An Empty Box for McNamara," *Far Eastern Economic Review*, Dec. 28, 1979, p. 40.

21. U.S., Congress, House, Committee on Foreign Affairs, 96th Cong., 1st sess., *Congress and Foreign Policy, 1978* (1979), p. 137.

22. "For Your Information: The Helms Amendment," United Nations Association of the United States of America, Dec. 1978.

23. U.S., Congress, House, *Congressional Record*, 95th Cong., 2nd sess., Sept. 29, 1978, pp. H11172, H11173.

24. "Statement by President Carter," Office of the White House Press Secretary, Oct. 10, 1978.

25. Editorial about the Helms Amendment, *Chattanooga Times*, Oct. 23, 1978.

26. Kurt Waldheim, "Financial Emergency of the United Nations," UN General Assembly, 33rd session, agenda item 103, Nov. 17, 1978.

27. Department of State incoming telegram, Jan. 13, 1979.

28. Ibid.

29. Hon. Benjamin Rosenthal, *Congressional Record*, Sept. 24, 1974, p. H32425.

30. Ibid., p. H32430.

31. *Public Papers of the Presidents of the United States: Jimmy Carter, 1978* (Washington, D.C.: Office of the Federal Registrar, 1979), 2:1636.

32. Max H. Kampelman, "Congress, the Media, and the Press," in *Congress against the President*, ed. Harvey C. Mansfield, Sr. (New York: Praeger, 1975), p. 88.

33. Rosenthal, *Congressional Record*, Sept. 14, 1974, p. H32435.

34. Whalen, ibid., July 24, 1975, pp. H24487–88.

35. "Turkey: U.S. Pact Now Dead," *Washington Post*, Aug. 3, 1975, p. A21.

36. Editorial, "Turkey: The Limits of Pressure," *Washington Post*, Oct. 12, 1975, p. C4.

37. *Middle East*, June 1975, p. 56.

38. *Flight International*, May 6, 1978, p. 1368.

39. Harold Wilson, *A Personal Record: The Labour Government, 1964–1970* (Boston: Little, Brown, 1974), p. 23.

40. Ibid., p. 25.

41. *America's African Policy*, Report of the First African-based Conference of African and American Representatives, Lusaka (African-American Institute, Jan. 1972), p. 26.

42. "U.N. Unit Condemns Rhodesia Trade Tie," *New York Times*, July 29, 1972, p. A5.

43. "U.N. Condemns U.S. in Rhodesia Trade," ibid., Dec. 8, 1972, p. A5.

44. *Africa 1974: Turning Points in America's Policy—Report, Fourth African American Dialogue* (African-American Institute, Dec. 1973), pp. 13–14.

45. Hon. William Frenzel, *Congressional Record*, 94th Cong., 1st sess., Sept. 25, 1975, p. H30224.

46. Hon. John Buchanan, ibid., p. H30235.

47. *Public Papers of the Presidents: Gerald Ford, 1976–1977* (Washington, D.C.: Office of the Federal Registrar, 1978), 2:1341–42.

48. Ibid., Sept. 15, 1976, 3:2256.

49. Hon. Richard Ichord, *Congressional Record*, Aug. 2, 1978, pp. H7730–32.

50. David Ottaway, "Africans Warn U.S. on Rhodesia," *Washington Post*, July 23, 1978, p. A1.

51. Zambia statistics obtained during Department of State telephone inquiry, Aug. 19, 1980.

52. *America's African Policy, 1972 Report*, p. 35.

53. U.S., Congress, House, 96th Cong., 2nd sess., *Foreign Assistance Legislation for FY 1981 (Part 9): Mark-up before Committee on Foreign Affairs, 1980*, p. 227.

54. "Conference of Tlatelolco: Declaration and News Conference," *Department of State Bulletin* 70, no. 1812 (Mar. 18, 1974): 263.

55. Ibid., p. 265.

56. "Message to Congress Transmitting 4th Annual Report on U.S. Foreign Policy," *Public Papers: Nixon*, May 3, 1973, p. 472.

57. "Special Message to Congress Proposing Trade Reform Legislation," ibid., April 10, 1973, p. 266.

58. Robert A. Pastor, "Coping with Congress's Foreign Policy," *Foreign Service Journal*, Dec. 1975, pp. 15–23.

59. *Keesing's Contemporary Archives*, Jan. 6, 1975, p. 26996.

60. Ibid.

61. "Latins, Upset over Trade, Postpone Talks with U.S.," *New York Times*, Jan. 28, 1975, p. 8.

62. "President Lopez of Colombia Makes State Visit to U.S.: Toast," *Department of State Bulletin* 73, no. 1895 (Oct. 20, 1975): 592.

63. *Public Papers: Ford*, April 10, 1975, 1:467.

64. "U.S. and Panama Reestablish Diplomatic Relations: OAS Announcement," *Department of State Bulletin* 50, no. 1296 (April 27, 1964): 656.

65. "U.S. and Panama Agree on Principles for New Canal Treaty," *Department of State Bulletin* 70, no. 1809 (Feb. 25, 1974): 187.

66. U.S., Congress, House, *Congressional Record*, 94th Cong., 1st sess., June 26, 1975, pp. H20945, H20946, H20948.

67. *Foreign Broadcast Information Service: Daily Reports*, Latin America, June 20, p. N1.

68. Ibid.

69. "Panama Apologizes for Youths' Attack on U.S. Embassy," *Washington Post*, Sept. 25, 1975, p. A34.

70. *Public Papers: Carter*, Aug. 8, 1977, 2:1462–63.

71. Ibid., pp. 1453–54.

72. Crabb and Holt, *Invitation to Struggle*, p. 75.

73. Foreign Affairs Committee, *Congress and Foreign Policy, 1979* (1980), p. 108.

74. Hon. George Hansen, *Congressional Record*, 96th Cong., 1st sess., Sept. 20, 1979, pp. H8249–50.

75. *Foreign Broadcast Information Service*, Sept. 24, 1979, p. N2.

76. Ibid., Sept. 27, 1979, p. N1.

77. Ibid., Sept. 29, 1979, p. N1.

78. Hon. Robert Bauman, *Congressional Record*, 96th Cong., 1st sess., Sept. 16, 1979, p. H8514.

79. "Canal Zone No More," *Tribune* (Scranton, Penn.), Oct. 4, 1979.

80. *Public Papers: Ford*, Oct. 30, 1975, 2:1758.

81. U.S., Congress, House, *Congressional Record*, 96th Cong., 1st sess., April 9, 1979, p. H2077.

82. Hon. Edward Derwinski, "Dear Colleague Letter," May 22, 1980.

83. U.S., Department of State, *Proposed Program for Syria, FY 1981*, April 1980.

84. "Baathists Urging Syria to Bolster Moscow Alliance," *Washington Post*, Aug. 23, 1980, p. A16.

85. Loren Jenkins, "Syria Agrees to a Merger with Libya," *Washington Post*, Sept. 3, 1980, pp. A1, A16.

86. Hon. Jonathan Bingham, *Congressional Record*, 94th Cong., 2nd sess., Sept. 10, 1975, p. H28306.

87. Arthur Schlesinger, Jr. "Human Rights and the American Tradition," *Foreign Affairs* 57, no. 3 (1979): 513.

88. Abraham Lowenthal, "The Human Rights Issue: Some Good Things Are Happening," *Los Angeles Times*, July 27, 1980, p. V2.

89. Emigration figures obtained during telephone interview with State Department employee, June 20, 1980.

90. Charles A. Krause, "Argentina Bars Grain Curb," *Washington Post*, Jan. 26, 1980, p. A17.

91. Hon. Donald Fraser, "Human Rights and U.S. Foreign Policy: Some Basic Questions regarding Principle and Practice," *International Studies Quarterly* 23, no. 2 (June 1979): 185.

92. Jonathan Power, "Carter's Human Rights Policy: Half-Filled Canvas," *Washington Post*, Aug. 29, 1980, p. A30.

93. Lowenthal, "Human Rights Issue," p. V2.

94. Author's conversation with Hon. Charles Vanik on Sept. 5, 1980.

95. Personal interview with Hon. Thomas P. O'Neill, June 20, 1980.

96. William E. Griffith, "Congress is Wrecking Our Foreign Policy," *Reader's Digest*, Feb. 1976, p. 72.

CHAPTER 6

1. Richard F. Fenno, Jr., *Congress in Committees* (Boston: Little, Brown, 1973), p. 1.

2. David R. Mayhew, *Congress: The Electoral Connection* (New Haven: Yale University Press, 1974), pp. 5–6, 49–65.

3. Lawrence Dodd, "Congress and the Quest for Power," in *Congress Reconsidered*, ed. Dodd and Oppenheimer (New York: Praeger, 1976), pp. 271–72.

4. Morris P. Fiorina, *Congress: Keystone of the Washington Establishment* (New Haven: Yale University Press, 1977), p. 46.

5. U.S., Congress, House, 96th Cong., 2nd sess., Continuation of Hearings before the Subcommittee on Treasury, *U.S. Postal Service Appropriations*, March 17, 1980. The House post office estimates that for every piece of incoming mail there are four outgoing parcels from members' offices.

6. Neal Gregory, "Broadcasting and the House," draft manuscript prepared for the Committee on House Administration, Sept. 30, 1980, pp. 1, 2, 7, 8, 9, 11, 12.

7. George H. Gallup, *The Gallup Poll: Public Opinion, 1972–1975*, (Wilmington, Del.: Scholarly Resources, 1978), 3:241.

8. Gallup, *Gallup Poll*, Oct. 12, 1978, p. 248.

9. Barry B. Hughes, *The Domestic Context of American Foreign Policy* (San Francisco: Freeman, 1978), p. 199.

10. Ibid., p. 96.

11. Aage R. Clausen, *How Congressmen Decide: A Policy Focus* (New York: St. Martin's, 1973), p. 225.

12. Hamilton Subcommittee on Investigations, *Hearings on Congress and Foreign Policy*, statement by Hon. Thomas E. Morgan, June 29, 1976, p. 91.

13. Personal interview with Hon. Timothy Wirth, June 25, 1980.

14. Randall B. Ripley, *Congress: Process and Policy* (New York: Norton, 1979), p. 216.

15. William Stimson, "Fighting Foley by Fair Means and Foul," *Argus*, April 28, 1975, pp. 1, 6, 13.

16. Campaign literature of Oct. 27, 1978, and newspaper advertisement in the *Spokane Review*, Spokane, Washington, Nov. 5, 1978, p. A11, paid for by Alton for Congress Committee, D. Braitwait, treasurer.

17. Ward Sinclair, "Special-Interest Shock Troops: All Out War," *Washington Post*, Oct. 25, 1980, p. A4.

18. Nick Thimmesch, "A Campaign Ruckus over Charges of Anti-Semitism," syndicated article, Oct., 1980, distributed by the *Los Angeles Times*.

19. Letter authorized by Sixth District Committees for Better Representation in Congress, Birmingham, Alabama, Sam N. Cole, chairman, Mar. 22, 1978, p. 2.

20. *Voting Scorecard for John Buchanan*, campaign literature paid for by Smith for Congress, Sam N. Cole, chairman, 1978.

21. *John B. Anderson Voted . . .* , political literature paid for by Friends of Don Lyons, John Johnson, chairman, 1978.

22. *Chris Dodd's Record of Shame*, political literature paid for by You Can't Afford Chris Dodd Committee, Dana J. Andrusik, executive director, Feb. 1, 1980.

23. Robert W. Lee, "Morris Udall: Why Arizona's Far Left Congressman Is Now in Deep Trouble," *Review of the News*, July 2, 1980, pp. 41, 43.

24. Edward Bruske, "The Making of an Issue," *Washington Post*, Oct. 21, 1980, pp. C1, C3.

25. Edwin M. Yoder, Jr., "Richardson Preyer and the Pursuit of Excellence," *Washington Star*, Jan. 1, 1981, p. A23.

26. *The National Taxpayers Union Rates Congress: Congressional Spending Study, 96th Congress, 2nd Session, 1980*, pamphlet distributed by National Taxpayers Union, Washington, D.C., 1980.

27. Bill Keller, "Congressional Rating Game Is Hard to Win," *Congressional Quarterly Weekly Report*, Mar. 21, 1981, p. 512.

28. *For the Record*, political advertisement paid for by Ed Weber Congressional Committee, Toledo, Ohio, July 1980, p. 7.

29. *Congressman Tony Hall Admits His Votes Caused Inflation*, campaign advertisement paid for by Sealy for Congress Committee, 1980.

30. "Ugly Politics Hurts Us All," *Dayton Daily News*, July 6, 1980, p. 14.

31. John W. Kingdon, *Congressmen's Voting Decisions* (New York: Harper and Row, 1973), p. 59.

32. William D. Rogers, "Who's in Charge of Foreign Policy?" *New York Times Magazine*, Sept. 9, 1979, p. 49.

CHAPTER 7

1. Woodrow Wilson, *Congressional Government* (Cleveland: Meridian Books, 1969), p. 76.

2. Hon. William Frenzel, "House Reforms and Why They Haven't Worked," *Commonsense*, winter 1980, p. 45.

3. Personal interview with Hon. Lucien Nedzi, June 26, 1980.

4. J. William Fulbright, "The Legislator as Educator," *Foreign Affairs* (spring 1979): 727.

5. Richard Bolling, *Power in the House: A History of the Leadership* (New York: Dutton, 1968), p. 16.

6. Catherine E. Rudder, "The Committee Reform and the Revenue Process," in *Congress Reconsidered*, ed. Lawrence C. Dodd and Bruce I. Oppenheimer (New York: Praeger, 1976), p. 138.

7. Information regarding the 1979–80 Democratic Caucus meetings was extracted from caucus minutes, which Congressman Foley's office kindly made available.

8. U.S., Congress, House, 94th Cong., 2nd sess., *Congress and Foreign Policy*, Report of the Special Subcommittee (Hamilton Committee) on Investigations of the Committee on International Relations, Jan. 1977, p. 4.

9. Roger H. Davidson and Walter Oleszek, *Congress against Itself* (Bloomington: Indiana University Press, 1977), p. 203.

10. Richard L. Lyons and Helen Dewar, "On the Hill," *Washington Post*, April 29, 1980, p. A5.

11. James A. Robinson, *Congress and Foreign Policy Making* (Homewood, Ill.: Dorsey Press, 1967), p. 196.

12. *Congress and Foreign Policy*, p. 21.

13. U.S., Congress, House, *Congressional Record*, 96th Cong., 2nd sess., June 5, 1980, pp. H4564–65.

14. *Congress and Foreign Policy*, pp. 2, 7.

15. U.S., Congress, House, 94th Cong., 2nd sess., *Congress and Foreign Policy*, Hearings before Special Subcommittee on Investigations of the Committee on International Relations, July 20, 1976, p. 134.

16. Ibid., p. 137.

17. Personal interview with C. Williams Maynes, Mar. 24, 1980.

18. Robert G. Neumann, *Toward a More Effective Executive-Legislative Rela-*

tionship in the Conduct of America's Foreign Affairs (Washington: Center for Strategic and International Studies, Georgetown University, 1977), p. 27.

19. *Congress and Foreign Policy*, p. 11.

20. Neumann, *Toward a More Effective Executive-Legislative Relationship*, p. 29.

21. Information concerning Senator De Concini's protest was supplied by his staff assistant Jerry Bonhom in a personal interview, June 25, 1980.

22. Lloyd N. Cutler, "To Form a Government," *Foreign Affairs* 59 (fall 1980): 129, 131, 139, 140.

23. Richard F. Fenno, Jr., "Strengthening a Congressional Strength," in *Congress Reconsidered*, ed. Lawrence C. Dodd and Bruce I. Oppenheimer (New York: Praeger, 1976), p. 264.

24. Fulbright, "Legislator as Educator," p. 723.

25. Ibid.

26. Fenno, "Strengthening," p. 267.

27. Personal interview with Hon. Stephen J. Solarz, Feb. 12, 1980.

28. Speech delivered by Thomas Corcoran before the Washington chapter of the Harvard Business School Alumni Association at Kenwood Country Club, Bethesda, Maryland, Sept. 17, 1980.

29. Alfred Steinberg, *Sam Rayburn* (New York: Hawthorne, 1975), pp. 107–8.

30. Ibid., p. 109.

31. John Spanier and Eric M. Uslaner, *How American Foreign Policy Is Made* (New York: Holt, Rinehart and Winston / Praeger, 1978), pp. 166, 168.

32. James Sundquist, "Congress and the President: Enemies or Partners," in *Congress Reconsidered*, p. 236.

33. Frank Annunzio et al., "Dear Colleague Letter," "Greater Use of Modified Rule," Sept. 12, 1979.

34. William Holmes Brown, *Constitution, Jefferson's Manual, and Rules of the House of Representatives*, 96th Cong., 1st sess., 1979, p. 556.

35. Ibid., p. 525.

36. Hon. Herbert E. Harris II, "Dear Colleague Letter," "Legislating Responsibility: Limiting Legislation in Appropriations Bills," Oct. 16, 1979, p. 1.

37. Annunzio, et al., "Greater Use."

38. Bruce Oppenheimer, "The Changing Relationship between House Leadership and the Committee on Rules," paper delivered at Dirksen Congressional Leadership Research Center and Sam Rayburn Library Conference, Georgetown University Law Center, Washington, D.C., June 11, 1980, p. 14.

39. I. M. Destler and Thomas R. Graham, "United States Congress and the Tokyo Round," *World Economy* 3, no. 1 (June 1980): 69.

40. U.S., Congress, House, *Congressional Record*, 96th Cong., 1st sess., Oct. 19, 1979, p. H9422.

41. Annunzio, et al., "Greater Use."

42. Harry Ammon, *James Monroe: The Quest for National Identity* (New York: McGraw-Hill, 1971), p. 394.

Index

☆ ☆ ☆ ☆ ☆